Teconomic Analysis of Millennial Economies

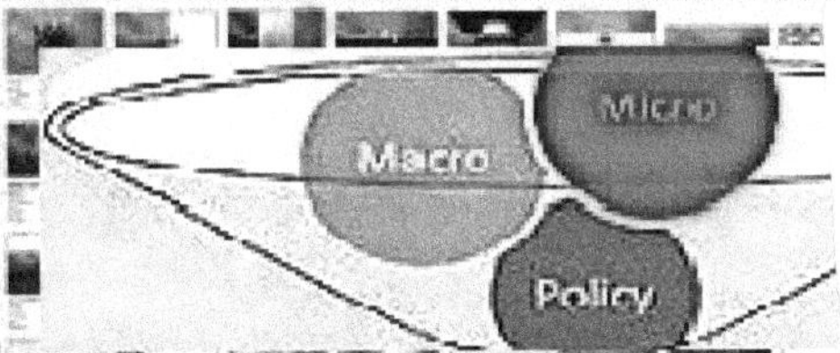

Teconomics Of Millennial Economics

Bahman Fakhraie, PhD

for mass distribution
not disturbance

All New
Insecurities
Super Duper ~~Securety~~
For you only

Dr. Bahman Fakhraie © 2017

TECONOMICS OF MILLENNIAL ECONOMIES

Teconomics of Millennial Economies

Teconomic Analysis
Of Modern Political Economic Issues

By

Bahman Fakhraie, PhD.

July 7, 2017

Back cover picture : The Weaver House Portland Or.

Front and back cover, FERDAT
FERDAT Publishing, Ogden, UT, USA
Published in Untied States of America
Library of Congress
Case #: 15660607601
ISBN: 978-0-9966334-6-8

$80.00
ISBN 978-0-9966334-6-8
58000>
9 780996 633468

DEDICATION

To Kay Davis, Lara Fatemeh, Anayat Wayne.

I also appreciate my extended family in Dezful Iran, which has expanded globally. You are in our hearts; do not be discouraged (Viva le Familia). This is dedicated to all generous, kind, and hospitable people, globally. Whence each job well done, each extended hand in help, in friendship, in charity, or in education is the proof that the gifts of all deities are in our human hearts, when used appropriately. I thank many friends here in United States. All readers with new technologies, especially book readers, they have truly found the lights in the darkness of life, do not let it go out, for all children of humanity, they will need it even more than our generations did. Our parents, family members, great teachers, and scholars have passed away. In memoriun, they remain in our thoughts with thanks.

ABSTRACT

This research is an accumulation of many years of analytical empiricism and academic studies in economic fields. The focus in national wealth creation does not advance formulaic personal greed, hubris, profiteering. It present national mass dynamic wealth creation by job creation, livable wages, and positive rates of circularity of money for majority of nations, which supports economic growth in both arenas of national demand and supply, government and private sectors of the same economies. These are not mutually exclusive processes subject to partisans' entertainment, but they are balancing, and yes, dynamically balancing and punishingly recursive equations.

A better strategic development path will contain these new production factors, and production functions, which will meet three fundamental conditions. Lemma 1, is it necessary? Lemma 2, is it sufficient? Lemma 3, is it sustainable? Since the advancement of the second-best theorem, in complex optimization formulation in welfare economic theory, this part of authors' prominent studies advances the economic science toward sustainability condition.

Economies do make comebacks and get through bad times, since they function with dynamic cyclical fluctuation, and if reparatory real disposable income redistributive adjustments through employments, are not replaced with regulatory wealth-concentrations, inadvertently or mischievously. However, it is important that one shift understand they are working on the same construction of the same building, and both shifts have to do their job of maintenances perfectly and without subterfuges, in order to be reemployed for the next job.

TABLE OF CONTEN

FIGURES

Figure Page

PREFACE

Different element of this book started at different time, but the motivation came to me, when the first millennial economic down turn did not act normally to mostly monetary stimuli, but it jumped after President Bush social security number few hundred dollars fiscal injection. In some early writing in 1970s, about dynamic adjustments in the rate of growth of GDP in response to money supply adjustment, I was interested, in the unilateral inflection that a monetary-policy-alone will have in a depression type of sticky downturn.

Usually political nature of fiscal policy makes it theoretically more responsive to economic stress. However, if you wait long enough all things become possible. Recent dysfunctional episodes in last years, gave me an opportunity to finish one of my earliest economic copyrighted papers, in this and in some earlier books. In the meantime, my eclectic background experiences in two continents, my research about some other continents, and the few other books in technology I wrote over the last two decades, gave me the holistic visions and the innovational clusters to finalize these works.

It turns out extremism is a vice, with consequences. It depends at which end of it one falls, as victims or victimizers. But the economic consequences of the negative externalities, such game theories generate are also greatly inclusive to victims and victimizers. Political parties, which indulge in extremism, mostly by the inexperienced gamers, operators, and politicians for populism sake, they will mature to regret the consequences. Therefore, they become marginalized as well.

When time has aged you,
And the youth have fled

Not even a mystic can divine you,
The mysteries of age

When beauty has passed, and grace is in your head,
And compassion has fled

Not even a mystic can divine you,
The mysteries of life

(Continues)

§§§§

CHAPTER 1

THE MILLENIAL ECONOMICS

While there are increasingly fewer reasons to abandon all hope, and run nihilistically back into the wilderness of ignorance. There are often a few hard bumps to consider. After the few dead bounces in the down ward cascades of the 2008-2009, the great contraction of 2008, the second of the new millennium, we need to study the whole economy for longer-term remedies.[1] The executive suits' solution, and the mega bank monopolies have been self-serving and non-productive, not a surprise to global kin observers.

The newer billionaires' model will serve the same economic cold dish harshly. Feed the failures strategies produced bigger failures in the supply sides. They may have had a little help from the neocons, and induced global events, but it is not apparent that they have learned any lessons from their failures.

The Declines

The millennial economic events were not all created on the day the calendar turned. There have been negative currents, instead of combined efforts globally, or regionally. It is inclusive of positive externalities to push or adopt austerity as part of a constructive futuristic plan package to maintaining economic growth based on shared increasing livable real disposable incomes across all economic classes and income levels.

However, it is quite different, when it is a political agenda, mixed with overt racial overtones, anti-women politics, anti-minority agenda, a southern strategy push against all immigrants and some minorities, and a vehicle of war profiteering for foreign intrigues and opportunism. Add the sustained push to long wars past democratic market economies toward dystopian resource striping for wealth concentration for a limited economic class, or just the billionaires' subclass. Then, the beneficiaries of the same plan undermine the tax revenues. In return, they want to fee and tax the middle class, cut the education of their children, social security, and Medicare of their retiring parents, while they are cutting their jobs and retraining of middle class and poor students, and continue to transfer tax-breaks to the top one percent income earners. That is not a plan for prosperity. It is a recipe for economic catastrophes.

This is not conservatism, which they teach in academic institutions, or history book. It explains why they do not like the educators. It is SCHADENFREUDE. It is an abstractionist strategy for deconstruction, instabilities, and economic unsustainable imbalances, mixed with enjoyment obtained from the troubles of others.

It has garnished substantial negative externalities nationally, and even more, internationally. It is cascading, and the systems have folded a few times. It is not a good recommendation for futuristic leaderships, which like to advance American exceptionalism. However, in honest and functional democracies, the voters will decide, the government they deserve, and they have to pay for it.

Demand flow constrictions are more systemically inlaid in this economic misconstruction, they were systemic profligates to finance the executive suits and supply-side religions, and bleed the working middle class, students, teachers, airline industry workers, and working poor, middle class, and small firms. The implosions of the financial super-infrastructure, from the made sausages of new <investment?> instruments, were faster than they could explain them rationally, even after the fact. These were the worst timed global economics' catastrophes of the human history.

This long in the making freak-shows came with most ample warnings about securitizations, derivatives, instrument risks, credit-risks quality and packaging (credit swaps, and derivatives), and about trust in the market mechanism of all times 1995, 1998, 2001, 2003, 2006, 2008. These had the potential of economic depression level melt down. They had so many bells, lights, and vessels on it to make it gaudier than a Louisiana gambling steamboat on a fat-Tuesday night loaded with drunken customers of all denominations! These included top advisers, a fed chairperson, and others. Well, mistakes were made! Brothers and sisters, can I hear a Halleluiah? Can I hear a Takbir? Oh, just say Bismellah. Amen will do just fine.

Tax breaks for the Few, More Taxes and Fees for the Middle-Class America. The most dishonest squeals about executive pay limitation, tax breaks for the rich as job-creation have reached a media crescendo, it seems they starting to believe their own lies. They say these are the causes of three-decade long demand-flow constrictions. These are amusing grease piglet grabs and squeals. Nevertheless, they are systemic proof of dishonest prices-wages-tax value linkages, which we need to break, and reset, even in the sub-conscience of the handpicked board members, and executive-suits, and their bondage-political parties globally.

The depression was due to the republicans shifting the income tax and fee burdens from the top so called top one –percent industrialists to the immigrants, then the poor and working Americans (white, black, or purple Americans, student and teachers), elderly and school age Americans, and finally the middle-class. Just to prove their intentions, as soon as, they controlled the executive, and legislative branch both houses, they went back to lock and seal the billionaires' tax break deals, cutting healthcare, Medicare, and earned benefits.

Figure 1 shows adjusted growth income of top 5, 10, and bottom 50 percent per capita 1987-2009.[2]

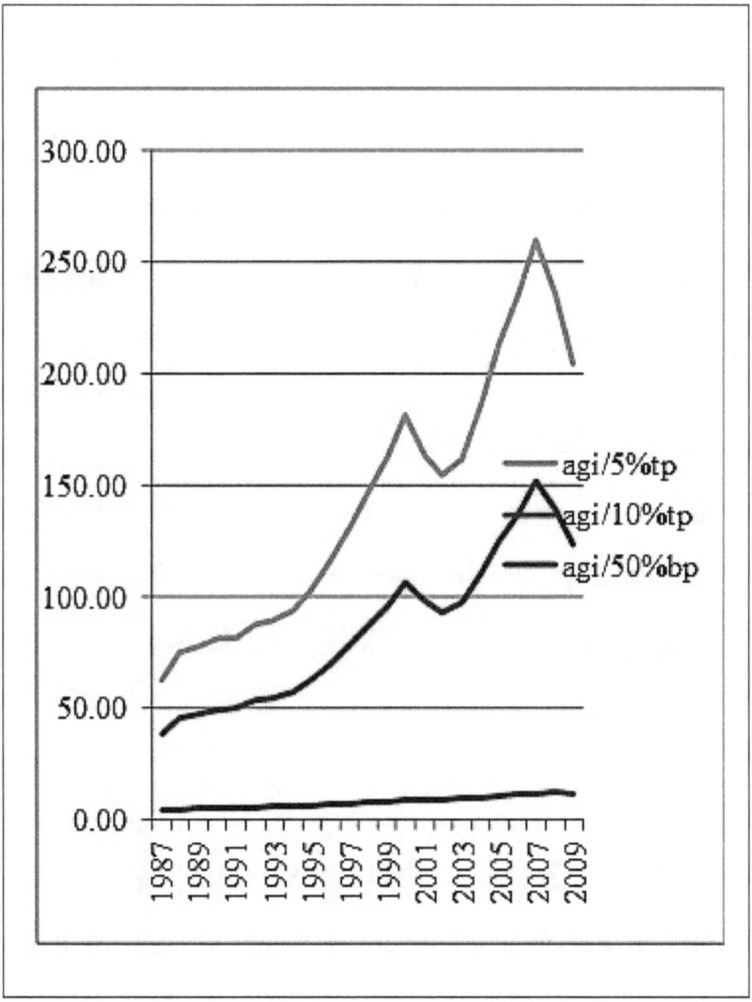

Figure 1, Adjusted growth income of top 5, 10, and bottom 50 percent per capita 1987-2009.

They paid for the income tax drop of the rich and mega cooperation, from effective rates 55 percent to 25 percent. Nevertheless, the hedge funds managers, and CEOs found their way to pay 15 percent, 12 percent, zero, or negative rates.[3] The 15 percent is the capital-formation tax rate, which was designed for investment and low-income ladder, but not infrastructure wrecking tax heaven for mega billionaires.

Moreover, some incorporated entities use tax laws to reduce their effective rates lower to zero. Because, the legislations are tweaked, amended, and if all else fails, earmarked, and changed in late hours. Then, they show up as austere mother superiors on prime time. They bankrupted the FDR, social security lock-box reducing the social security tax rate of the richest 1percent to zero (over $100,000.00), but axed the means-testing clause, for the multiple dippers-billionaires. That was socialism, or too pink to consider. Then, by blocking rational education policies, and hiring the graduates, and adequate retired workers' replacement by a moral and adequate immigration-policy, replacing welfare-recipients retraining projects with cooperate welfare, and tax-break for billionaires, they have boxed the economy in a dynamic but typically unsustainable wreck.

These were Republican Party designed to appease the billionaires, the cooperate entities into job-creation. Their supply side economic model has not created the jobs. So now, they need new blames, fresher scarecrows, new wars, elderlies Medicare, earned benefits, emigrant children healthcare, or student loan traps, and education cuts.

Instead, we have xenophobic hate mongering hodgepodge of anti-institutionalisms, and supremacies' irrationalism. The illegal menageries dressed up like immigration laws, which operates like high school skinheads' pledge to nickel and dime legal immigrants, storekeepers, restaurateurs, educators, students, and scholars to give up their hard earn chance at citizenship and self deport. Or the small businesses pay to play schemes, especially if they want or need to hire immigrants to operate. Since, the neo-slavery days, the peonage laws, and Dred Scott supreme court decision, the right wing-nuts are gifting historical dips to America again, with unending verbiages.

Ignoring that the immigrants by default are the only chance at the jobs-creation that some American workers will ever have, since industrialist capital investments are going to oversee and to global cheaper workers, or the technological mechanization, robotization, and unsustainable wages.

Americans cannot forget, they are in the age of technological displacements and cooperate- minimization of human laborer. Small and medium size job creators left are majority immigrants or related. Of course government jobs and jobs-creation are essential but taboos to confused polemicists of alt-right. The free market mantra of Milton Friedman age cannot be twisted to the extremists' contortions the alt-right wishes and prays.

They presented the immigrants as the supply side problem of labor and labor unions. What we saw in Wisconsin and other state with the Republican governors were not love and protection of union's wages and jobs, labors, education, or a sane immigration policy for legal immigrant. It was wedge issues to divide and rob them of their pensions, earned workers' and elderly benefits, and economically sustainable salaries. Citizen united decision of the high Court, was the first test of dysfunctional representations. They could have easily remedied the cash for law payola. They did not.

We are not even close to being out of economic difficulties. CEOs, managers are not capitalists. They are salaried workers with access to capital, the benefiters of capital–income flow, like shareholders, like workers, and like society by reasonable taxes of the larger income-flow (over 250ks, and 500ks). The larger executive pays should be studied for appropriate tax rates, until then or for now, a universal cap need to be put in place, which covers all academic institutions, health facilities, military and quasi-state cooperation, and private publically sold cooperation. Until and unless there are fundamental repairs in the unemployment-data indices improvements up to three to five years in employment (and not the temporary workers, internships, fraudulent employment indices).

Moreover, until we have higher real national average salaries. The talk of taxpayers' money (TARP, stimulus-funds) going to these un-necessary and self-delusional high-executive pays beyond $500,000 is beyond pale of any logical decency, it is rewarding failures and the most anti-capitalistic politically dishonest acts possible.

This mid-plight of the current potential-depression, regardless how short it lives, we have lost more than 50 percent of values around us. Some 2000 points drop and over two trillion dollars evaporations are common. We need to correct the market infrastructures. Any new legislation slices and dices the taxpayers need to include a ten-year claw back.

There is a good reason why broker-bankers with broken-business models got in the payday type of rate usury, robots' signings, and rate jacking, contract breaking Modus Operandi.[4] Because robbery is, too much work, and does not pay as well. The thieveries, the money exchange rates, the usury was not affecting the rich, and they needed cash to cover what they CEO salaries would take out of the business operation. Unfortunately, this cooperate imbecilic broken-business model has been adopted by most, if not all corrupted greedy executives from private to public schools, universities executive suits, and volunteer originations globally.

All of the religious politicians were in on the swindles, for small reelection-gratuities, but do not call it payola, or bribe. Some honest executives had self-initiated $1 salaries, knowing cooperate accounts pay for transportations and all operational expenses, but they have children in college and expense too (mindful of accumulated student loans ballooning). If they want to start their own hedge fund and bring down the USA-markets as they did in September 08, February 09, August 11, new tick-up federal laws and interim breaks in market downs at 10 percent down ticks will put an end to that. These corrections would have helped since last spring, if the laws were there! You either help us all crawl out of these hells of honey wells you created, or we will use your high-income taxes as the stepping-stones to create the jobs, you forgot you promised.

Economic Trauma

Our legislators (state and federal) have been part of myriads of misplaced convoluted regulations, which have taken away from market-trust and added to alienations and nonparticipation in the markets, globally.

The saddest twisted attempts to blame the immigrants, and minorities, and disguising xenophobic, racists, sexists' laws under patriotic fervors, or mistaken economic necessities, or false crime fighting provosts have not slowed these depression butt-slides and drag-downs, one iota. As busy beavers and killer bees, these idiocies and imbecilities have costs us much international moral high grounds, international leadership, the sense of global self-respect, and striped us of energetic workers at the middle and bottom of human capital.

Some of the red states (republican dominated states) have started to fleece and attack teachers, police, fire workers, low and middle-income workers, and reap them off their salary increases to show belatedly how conservatives they are. All the while, they are conceding economic positions to competitors. These only expedited the 30-year predesigned-perdition on the middle class and working poor, thus a self-destructively induced technology-steroidal depression in the domestic demand-side economics is being created dynamically. Further, these will be depressing the already robbed economy out of the demand-fuel, which it needs to grow. Then we cannot be surprised, when Chinese, German, and other economies pull out of depression faster, and we are looking forward to a W, or V then U or a long U, double dip, in the growth rates of our GNP, here and there, before any recovery!

It is not surprising, that there is a resistance to study these dishonest forays in illogic infamy of self-destructions, of illegalities, of war criminalities, and torturing illogicalities, the so-called Wall Street investment big-banks' Ben-Ladinism attacks on the main streets fester.

Ten-year claw backs may not help there, but corrective reconstruction instead of do-nothing legislations will make a difference. All bad laws enacted are in need of sunset-revisions, before any economic recovery reification, they are badly in need of nullification, they deserve. Otherwise, let us do the independent counsels institutional colon cleansing as you wish, then null and void these imbecilities.

Past and current investment Bank models are corruptively broken, the laws of separation between normal bank operations (in the big bad Banks' model) and their securitization formulation need revalidations, by independent prosecutors now (scientific or academic research initially, before their societal adaptations).

Mix securitizations of assets will need to be halted for now; otherwise, the assets will garnish the highest risks, and lowest values. For example, in real estate mortgages, the 30 years, low fixed mortgages cannot be bundled with sub-primes, arms and balloons, or any other assets, if these other kinds of mortgages need to exist at all! The credit rating agencies and original banks must share some of the damages, since they shared the big benefits. The executives, with extreme-pay packages, need to share in the pay back. They went along with the generated wrong rates, AAA, for CCC or junks. Only about 500 banks out 8500 should have not wrecked banking for the nation or the globe productive processes. They cannot be set free to redo the same harm. Nevertheless, voucher-aid, job-creations for loans has to replace, complement (TARP) and all other injections, tax credits, and tax breaks into supporting the banking super-infrastructure, or all cooperate-welfares, subsidies, major tax breaks, must have job retraining and job-creation clauses added to them.

A private asset clearing central operation, organization (PACO) needs new laws to be established. It cannot be as abusive as the (Real Estate Trust cooperation) RTC, of the saving and loans famed fiasco, which was a filter to return good assets back to the same institutions on top of the taxpayers' funds. PACO will need new permission to buy assets at par to 20 percent of par. The difference will become initial government loan-costs. They need to individualize and localize the asset class. Single family, rentals, malls, individual's shops, are not the same risk class in New York New York, and Mantua Utah. In addition, all assets have to be published or put on the internet for first come first serve bids, and for the transparency. HUD (Housing and Urban Dept.), and FHA (Federal Housing Agency), and any private mortgage company and banks can centralize the paperwork for 30-42 years fixed mortgages, or business loans to keep them honest. The temporal profit of each sale returns to taxpayers on the spot, by property taxes over time, and by asset sake taxes at the end of transactions. They will check out prequalification, qualification and banks letters of buyers. Transparency, fairness of access, and honesty in intends will calm nerves globally.

The temporal price arbitrage, adjustment will pick up after initial fed funds are reduces in a diminishing curve. PACO will only need a three to seven-year revisit to fund or close down. The private fund can be encouraged to take such a risk for two reasons. One: there is government backing. Two: there is profit in buying cleaned assets at 20-40 percent and selling them at 60-80 percent.

Homebuyers, shop owners, investors will buy cleaned assets from HUD, for three reasons. One: government gives quick-claim deeds. Two: Government guarantees, fairness, none discrimination and no-fraud clauses. Three: there is profit in temporal price arbitrage, or buying at 60 percent and selling at 80 percent, or higher.

Government normally do not want to hold on too long, because of the state and federal taxes on private revenue-stream generations are annual, like their government-costs of operations, which will be dynamically increasing in the longer run, greater than the temporal one time increases to most capital-asset increase (110 percent), after a long time holding.

Nationalization is a guaranteed lost for governments all around. Certain privatization can rejuvenate capitalism somewhat! There is another economic law that no one will teach. That monopoly-centralized business-model of the west mimics and implodes like the communists' elitisms and state-centralisms monopoly-business models of the East. That is economic theory at work, not the militarism, not jingoism, and cults of personalities of Keynes, Marx, Adam Smith, or anyone else. And, remember where you read it.

However, those who want to preach free markets need to respect perfect competitions' rules about informed market, reasonable price-wage-rent income and tax rate equilibriums and redistributions- prerequisite rationality, and accommodating regulatory moderations, and free flow of both capital and workers. The worst offenders lately are the so-called potentate-republicans on the taxpayers' tab for more than last fifteen years. If it is not income taxes, it is the state and property taxes, or sales taxes, or fees, as long as it is against the middle class, workers. Every time they have a free hand, they launch another xenophobic attack on the immigrants, workers, or capital markets, since their 1996 fiasco. Therefore, economies decline.

They are the reason we have intellectual capital flights, manufacturing flights, worker flights. When they attack another industry, part of agriculture economy folds, or manufacturing economy runs over seas, or the hospitality industries becomes inhospitable. It all has become accumulatively and negatively compounding, or punitively implosive. That is in the end we all do not just die, but at the end, we all get the bills. The days that political party idiots put sheets on their heads and went after legal immigrants, minority Americans, women that work for them, or employ them, or take care of their credit markets, or supply their energy is over! It never existed without many harms and self-harm and civil wars of one kind or another.

Those dangerous minds that seem to re-promote it will not go away, but they will have to be safely far-removed from all government seats, and in all states, and economies, which wish to be economically viable and functioning states. Their global trade-partners have told them so repeatedly, now their economic depression will remove the plugs out of their ears.

Governments need to responsively protect all people from predatory bad businesses, during economic down turns. Every time a Politian, or a representative comes on the sleepwalking media, they have to be asked beside higher benefit, free government healthcare for themselves, legal self-immunity of the laws they create, what they have done for the taxpayers, for the workers, for the middle class, small businesses, students, and teachers, police and fire persons, lately.

Usury laws need to be reestablished and enforced for any loan-interests over 13 percent unless in time of inflation above 13 percent. A penalty needs to be levied on offending institutions. Credit card rates of 6-8 percent need to be the rule not the exceptions for up to $10,000 loans. Credit bureau rating, numbering, scorings, if include three errors, need to be kept away for up to a year. Moreover, a penalty levied, partly it must pay for the damages it causes on victimized families of those customers. Predatory pay-day loans, other mushrooming check loans cannot go over the 12 percent per annum, rate at any time (0.12/365 (0.0004) per day), unless inflation rate temporarily exceeds 13 percent. These will require federal laws, because some states already have seen a twisted logic in profiteering off their poorest population by sale taxes, and usury interest rates, never-mind the commercial jail-houses and immigration-incarcerations profiteering-centers. These states are usually the states that fight living wage laws. Federal laws would preempt such states, which have already established (>100) percent interest on payday loans. A loan-life cap of 20 percent per annum, including interest, fees, fines, and penalties for credit cards' and day loans should become federal law. Revisiting the financial act of 1995 may also be advisable at these times.

Breach of Contracts

The worst offending abuse of all time, is manipulating student loans to profit milking machine, thus perverting a human capital production creation tool in a most usurious self-destruction by way of the money grabs. All student loans need to be refinanced at 2 percent, 1 percent, or 0 percent, until rate of graduation and student, getting in the colleges, and universities, and graduate-schools, and jobs reaches their proportion of the population.

All student loan over the three percent, need a principle readjustment and major downsizing. When, the unemployment-rates will be under four percent by then. Student rate out to zero out, when the state and federal jobs are not created and they are non-existent, and government can or will not create service jobs, or trainee jobs.

That is one social contract broken by the government, while they demand the full repayment of student loans. Every time, the loan rate is increased legislatively, it is a breach of original contract, there should be a principle down grade adjustment penalty, and reduction of termination-deadline to ten years, instead of 20 years, in that breach of contract. In real life, the court will dismiss all claims on breach of contracts; in addition, punitive damages and attorney's fees are awarded. Moreover, there are no plans to create jobs. Why the do-nothing legislative on behest of their wealthy owners are insisting on a carryover of principle and added interest charges of their victims' taxpayers and the students.

Normal business activities and purchases involving consumer borrowing have become as risky as entrepreneurial actions for greater profits, fundamentally due to mercurial job markets. The major error in judgments (ideological misapplications) has been equivocating ordinary people job-pool and capital as expugnable piggybanks to supplement the executive suits irrational total pays. Technological dislocation mainly due to computerizations of workers' skills assisted in these dishonest hodgepodges of mismanagements and the none-regulatory free for all. During the tax breaks of multibillion dollars salaries and wealth concentrations of the one percent, all promised jobs never showed, all promised job retraining vanished. All or most new jobs vanished and relocated. Index-paradox showed productivity jumped by leaps and bounces, and it disassociated from the real disposable income three-decade drag down. WHY, because the tinkle-down supply side model was broken and tilted to milk for the tax breaks, not for capital, but for the one percent upper income earners.

Economic Down Turn

These were the dangerous telltale signs of pending economic implosions in view. While three to six month jerks were celebrated as some innovational wonderments. The lifeblood of the economy drained out of the demand-side. Therefore, the psychological contractions have had very deep roots.

The radical changes to bankruptcy laws took common consumption-decisions or even individuals' Healthcare expenses to the higher risk level of Dickensian federal offences, oddly for the middle class and unemployed poor only. They joined the victims of student loan and payday loan offenders as the new cockeyed-elitists targets of the Stalinists' capitalism, or their new Alternative right political Leninism. The tax-transfer strategies target them and the middle class, elderly-earned benefits, for billionaires' tax breaks, disastrously. They have not been shy about.

Advanced technological capitalism, in Microsoft industries, or computer technology and internet based multi-billions of dollars industries are no longer enfant industries. They and the multi-billionaires, individuals and cooperate interties have to support the economy, by billionaires' tax-transfer strategies. Purring trillions of dollars in the bottomless pits, investing in fixed obsolete military assets, and cash hording cooperate offices do not get us closer to the 75 percent demand-side sustainable economic solution. Employed, properly paid workers, immigrants, graduates, elderly with their sufficient earned-benefits are the only people, which can do that domestically and globally.

It took USA three decades for FDR, and the opposition to get the USA out of the hard grasp of depression, with the Hooveristic opposition making it harder all along. The Hooveristic capitalists were acting as the current do-nothing abstractionists, billionaires' tax-break advocates, Alt-right extremists, and Neocons have been acting. There are precious few methods and minds, to speed it up, so it will take less time.

Good news is it can be achieved. However, major contractions to aggregate demands will curtail benefits to all, expansion of opportunities, more jobs, and better wages will expand the whole economy, increase revenue, and help to see a vanishing deficit. Since FDR days, we have been handed this fork in the road conundrum, again. We have taken the wrong road without learning its lessons. What is good about having graduated workers, if you keep making the same uneducated decisions, and stay in perpetual chronic structural joblessness?

Doing nothing, doing something dishonest, doing profiteering, dropped us here in this honey-well of history, back walks, butt drugging, or heads in the sky, individualism makes no contribution now, it does not make any political sense. We have to do some things right, we may as well start doing them now.

Compare to the Real Depression

President Barak Housing Obama promised us work ahead, that is what we are going to have, a lot of work ahead of all of us. Correcting legislative misadventures, motivating and replacing the do-nothing chants, are part of those hard works. No one should wish the USA, or global economy to fail. Unfortunately, that is not what the oppositionists had in mind. They have unloaded all job-creation strategy, and twisted every opportunity to uplift the economy, and rerouted every tax breaks for the middle class, to coddled the upper billionaires.

No one has said that American people cannot do these right deeds. Despite the jeers from the political, and media peanut-galleries, we need to put shoulder to the wheel and push onwards and upwards again, until normal times return. Luckily, they do return, for correct-collective decisions to create jobs.[5]

The United States economy has been here before, it has seen worst, and it had come out of it. This graph shows the growth and decay rate of real gross domestic product (RGDP).[6] The Value is the dollar index chained to (year 2000), and data is from 1929 to 2008.

It was not just 1929. We did it again between 1929-1935, and 1935-1940. Moreover, it sounds silly. Nevertheless, we repeated it again by 1945. We repeated the same mistakes, and ended up with the same economic whole declines. Somehow, after 1950s, we become wise beyond our age, and stopped heading our collective heads against the same wall, stopped acting crazy for a few decades. Those years are too far back, but the last few crashes are recent.

We have heard wild assessments and expertise by financiers' reporters, and political operatives about the depth of depression hyperbolae, which we are experiencing. The data beg to differ. It does not allow for childhood abstinences, and abstractionisms.

Figure 2 shows the comparative influences of 1920-1930s, versus recent economic down turns. Particularly the proportional impacts of 1930, post 1935, and 1945 were much more significant. Nevertheless, the repetition and the grip of economic down turns, are also alarming.

Comparative

Figure 2 shows economic decay or growth rates for years 1929 to 2008.

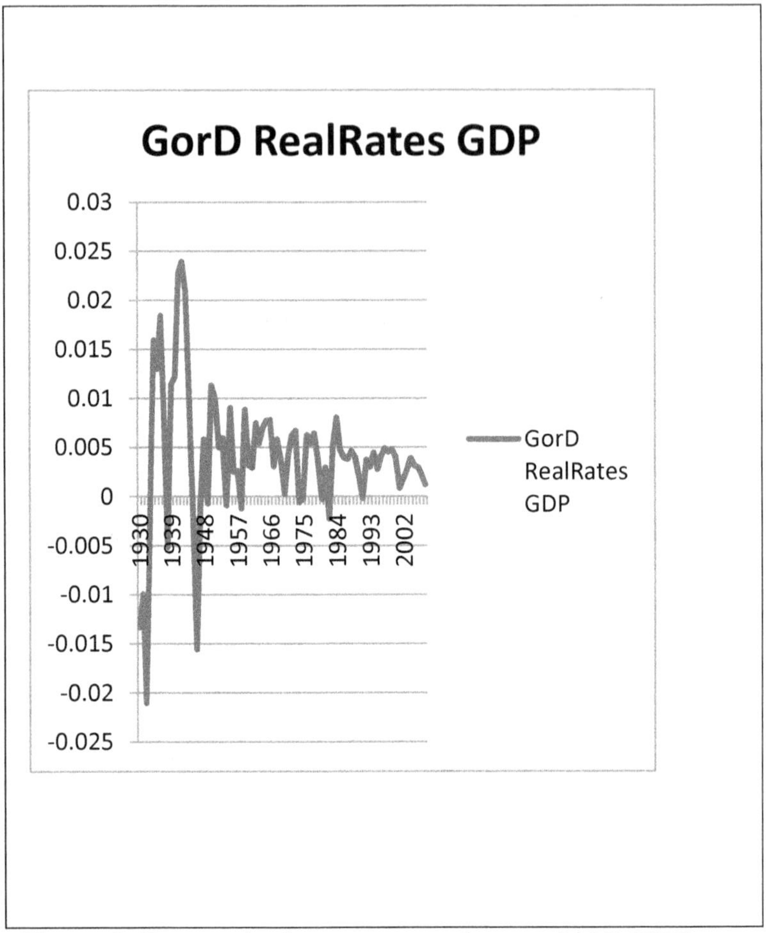

Figure 2, Economic decay or growth rates 1929-2008.

Study of timelines, of this decade with the depression decade will help seasoned comprehension.[7] Figure 3 shows comparative temporal 5 years interval-changes of real gross national products, 1929 and the 2000 decades, for five-year intervals.

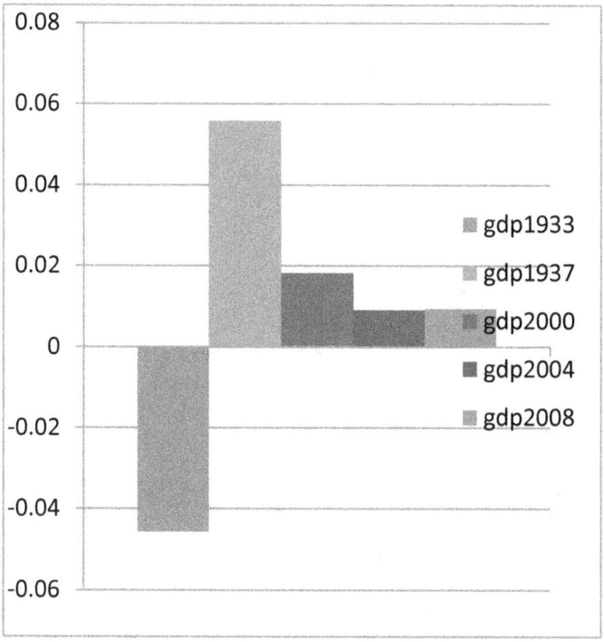

Figure 3, Comparative temporal 5 years decay and growth rate of real GDP.

Figure 4, shows a recent graph study of economic decay and growth cycles of USA economy.

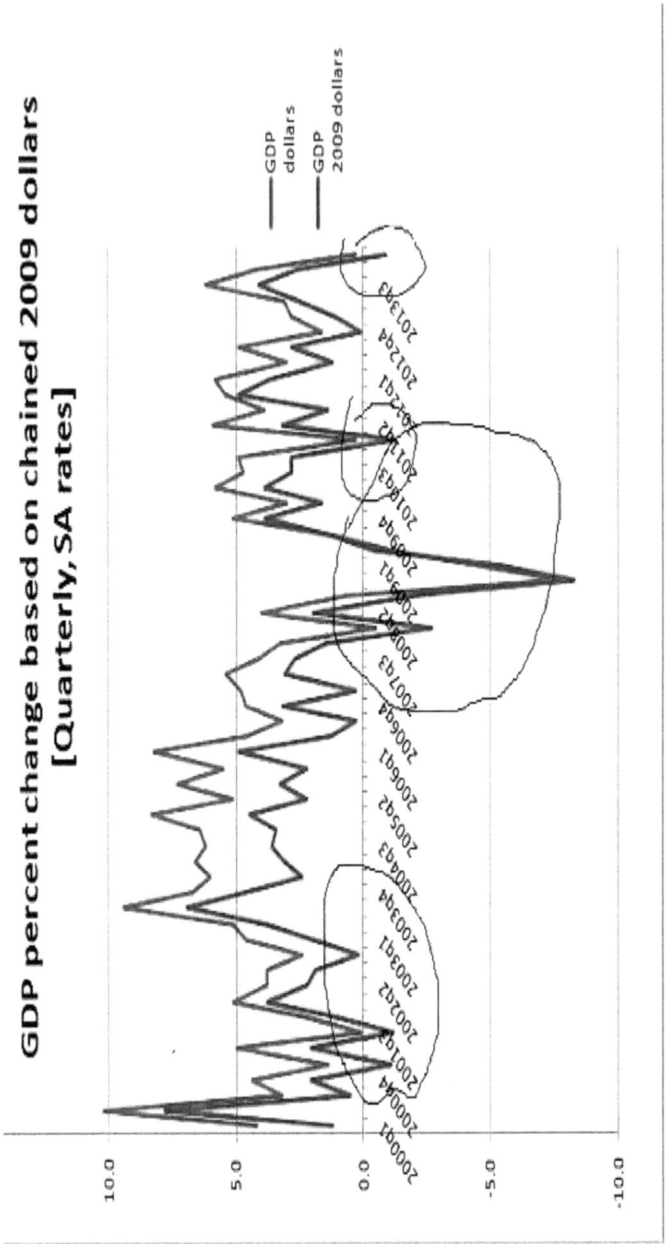

http://www.bea.gov/national/index.htm#gdp
Selection and graphing by Dr. Bahman Fakhraie c 2014

Figure 4. USA growth and decay of real GDP.

A lot of bipartisan adaptation of policies, and interventionism, remedied the huge first dive. However, those ubiquitous erroneous assumptive misjudgments, of the potentate self-interests of lobbyists, billionaires' cooperate-financiers still have their omnipresence and malignant influences on corrective macro policies. Therefore, the economy is not as bad as 1929 depression. However, even this millennial and more recent set of data and graph, and economic analysis show the increased frequency of the down cycles have a trend to them, which demands skilled attentions and further studies.

The study of employment data elucidates the structural issues, which have become deterministic. These areas of study are very important areas of concern, in job creation, political economics, and sane policy research and implementations for social and behavior scientists.

Notes

[1] There was a UN sponsored millennial development project, which had great merits. However, the broader influences of it have not progressed well.

[2] Table, 3 is part of the, "Adjusted Gross Income of Taxpayers in Various Income Brackets, 1980-2009 ($Billions)", in www.TaxFoundation.org. Population is assumed 303 mils, and per capita for 5, 10, and 50 percent is calculated by author. Also IRS.org, data is available for more detailed study.

[3] When we study tax expenditures, large numbers of cooperation receive government transfers, above tax their breaks, and beyond their capital-formation tax credits. That makes their effective tax rates negative. Most workers do not see those kinds of benefits.

[4] "Federal and state officials on Thursday announced a landmark $26-billion agreement with the nation's five largest mortgage servicers to settle investigations involving foreclosure abuses ...
for foreclosure paperwork problems and other improprieties by the servicers in the foreclosure process." Jim Puzzanghera, Mortgage giants to pay $26 billion in foreclosure settlement, *Los Angeles Times,* 7:02 AM PST

[6] U.S. Bureau of Economic Analysis, Survey of Current Business, April 2009,

<http://www.bea.gov/national/nipaweb /SelectTable.asp?Selected=N>.

[7] U.S. Bureau of Economic Analysis, http://www.bea.gov/National/Index.htm

U.S. Bureau of Economic Analysis, Survey of Current Business, April 2009. <http://www.bea.gov/national/nipaweb/SelectTable.asp? Selected=N>

CHAPTER 2

LESS PANICY CONUNBDRUMS

Now, we all live in interesting times, on this one Global Life Boat called earth. During the 2008 crash, and international banking crisis, Chancellor Angela Merkel and the German governments' Solution with Deutsche Bank and other German banks were not a beg-your-neighbor (BYN) policy. It is kicking your neighbors up the innovational step-latter policy, before Irish dew is lifted. Mr. Brown's of her majesty's government improved the package, with Italian government buying bank shares to inject liquidity and enhance credit markets, a lesser-socialized medicine solution, he said he had saved the world. We wished for a grander solution, or a permanent sustainable solution! Irish Banks' protection of depositors was also a backstop against cascading effect of vaporized trusts, confidence, and credits and liquidity out of the markets, after the paper-capital losses started to become realized misfortunes.

USA, UK, China, Russia, EU, and the global coordinated efforts are the kind of global positions in stormy waters, which encourage follow through by other decision makers, and eventually share buyers and captain of industry, unless thy perverse their courses to spreading regional conflicts. The credit-adjustments globally coordinated to increase its potency without (byn) issues, and calm and calculated none-panicky tech-injections have already taken place at the supply-side. Globally central banks or treasuries can coordinate and allocate up to 1 percent supply injection, a multi banks periodical GOLD dump, on the markets, can cool some of the speculative fevers out of the gold bobble.

A strong three-prong pincer support as initial remedies could have been injected on the demand-side, too.

Consumers, workers, middle class citizen, and all immigrants, they are invisible to the lobbyists, political neophytes, and luddites. Nevertheless, they are the other 75 percent of the economy. They will dictate the terms, duration, spring, and condition of the economy recovery. That is somewhat more of permanent solution. The total reliance on the supply side close system, zero sum game has been an unmitigated unchallenged disaster. It is a habitual response, because it worked in small recessions. Until the demand side is fixed, we will see these irregulars fallen down drunkard acts by the global markets, and near crash economies, a cascade effect step-downs, which the figure 2 showed.

The only problem left is commissar-Neocons that simultaneously vex ignorance and declare doom, gloom, hate, and rapture, then council long-wars, religious wars, and total- wars to remedy all ills, on televisions. In many ways, this has been a Neocon supply-side capitalism broken-model, which academic, and national science foundations, or none of the other foundations have been willing to finance the research to unlock the loot box. Unfortunately, like the "mien comp" book, teen green horns read it, and do more harm to themselves and everything around them. The Neocon supply-side capitalism broken-model is the Trojan horse model of modern economic choices. They have used it. They piggybacked the supply-side economical jargons, and just a smidgen of neoclassic economics, with nativism, and the patriotic fervors. They have traveled far undetected, with benighted certitudes. Their pet projects will rotate to knee capping the new administrations' assists to USA middle class, job creation, infrastructure rebuilding, and union salary and pension busting. On the other hand, they will stop any Job-creation stimuli from formation, in order to help the republican cabals to get in with the Neocons' hate, loathing, and long war agendas. That cannot be a logical

American agenda by choice. Therefore, the media cycle adds the cabalisms, with fear and loathing, big-sized portions.

The massive injection of uncertainty and risks are not healthy intellectual-pursuits for advanced economies now, stop them. Sooner than later, we will take them behind the wood-shed with their war and fear mongering foolish-friends, and the dishonest-greedy Executive pals, and terminate their services globally, so the rest of us mortals can reconstruct the functioning re-regulated free market free competition capitalisms and some functional democratic progress.

Workers and producers, teachers, police, firemen and women, farmers, movie-makers, screenwriters and gaffers, travel, hospitality, and entertainments industries, even honest bankers, investors and non-shifty executives, and very few rare-honest politicians (not always an oxymoron!) will work on through the difficulties, and some mega billionaires will help, they have been the leaders all along. People in America or Australia, or Middle East and Iran, and Africa, China, East Asia, and people from Moscow Russia to Masco Idaho, from Timbuktu Africa to tundra Alaska, USA and Canada have not given up on producing for their families or their countries. It is the idle, morbid, imbeciles screaming retirement-funds are gone, stocks have no value, sell all and go home, everyone is a terrorist or knows one, crash is here and good-life has ended in this or that country.

The global Chicken Little and chicken hawks, which have lost their senses, need to bow out gracefully! "The nattering nabobs of negativity,"[1] neocons need to ooze back under the kosher-rocks with their political lobbyists, moneychangers, and spend the rest of American taxpayers' foreign aid money. It ought to be the last they get, again. Unless you know something, try to be calm and quiet and carry on. Leave with grace, not with more lies and deceptive genocidal misconducts, or more war crimes! The global economies require constructional economic growth models, instead of destruction nihilisms.

Theater

This comedy of horrors can be explained in the language of movies, "what a stupendous catastrophe" from Kazantzakis's Zorba the Greek, staring Anthony Queen. We went past, IT IS A WONDERFUL LIFE staring Mr. James steward, to DELIVERENCE starring Mr. Burt Reynolds, and ONE FLOW OVER THE CUCKOO'S NEST, with Mr. Jake Nicholson. We have been experiencing TO KILL A MOCKINGBIRD staring Late Mr. Gregory Peck and Mr. Robert Duvall, and UNFORGIVEN starring Clint Eastwood, Gene Hackman, Morgan Freeman, and Richard Harris. After the few economic cyclical picks and troughs, we have ended up with HIGH ANXIETY starring Mel Brooks.

We temporary fixed the problems for 6 month in spring 2008. The consumers were left flat down and out again. Therefore, we ended up with THE GROUND HOGS' DAY with Mr. Bill Murray. In a tax-down and trickle tax breaks up model of class-war fare, which was not even done in the GODFATHER ONE, starring Mr. Marlon Brando, the middle class workers have been bamboozled. We just hope as in the movie Dracula with Bela Lugosi, or the newer one with Gene Wilder, the villagers will not have to get the torches and the pitchforks to chase out the republicans, to remind them of their constituency. After, their repeated national votes, for dissent Job-wage-tax redistribution, with good jobs and dissent real incomes for all Americans. So here, we are, with ANALYSZE THIS, and ANALYZE THAT, starring Mr. Robert De Nero, Mr. Billy Chrystal with the incomparable voice of maestro, the greatest singer of all time Mr. Tony Benet (Senior Antonio Benedetto), in perpetual wonderment.

Academia, Intelligentsia

The problem is the retraining-education funds, infrastructure funds (other than roads) went somewhere else, and so did the jobs. Most of the cash has gone to blowing minds and tearing up hearts in the Middle East. Moreover, the infrastructure has been faltering over and under us in USA. Of course, the movie production, movie making remains an integral part of any infrastructure recovery plans. If we fail to comprehend the expanded FDR vision of infrastructures, which in his days included Radio station and theatrical art productions, screenwriters, and writers, and agricultural land colleges, highly educated graduates, and expansive and expanding versions of Hollywood, we will fail to reconstruct the damaged economies. Unfortunately, some will employ radio-talk show artists instead of PhD economists for their business schools ethics and finance courses, and jack up student-loan costs, interest, and educational costs on the students. They will pay a little less, now. Nevertheless, we will sink back to shoveling money to broken down brokerage-bank models and crooked CEOs.

Post 1930's depression the petty fight on Keynesianism and parochial parsimonious thriftiness of Hoovers' broken business model delayed any kind of economic recovery two or three decades. It was when FDR team dropped all pretentious silly infightings and went all ought to hire and help employ all Americans, that sustainability crawled in and stayed. Some States, which failed to be inclusive, they took more than half of century to crawl back half way. They had all kinds of idiot historicism to back up their demented wrong turns, and nihilistically bent Southern strategies. They griped their religions, their guns, and the concrete blocks of intolerance, and sunk in their own dark waters of bigotries and hate mongering for a long time. They had defended trashing around on 10 to 20 percent of their functioning potential economy. That is all a southern strategy economic model can ever do for any economy. The Nazi model, the colonial model, the neocolonial, and now neocon models have been functioning on the same template. When they inevitably fail, they pick a minority other, and blame them for their failures. Now we still all have another good beginning, and all states are asking for financial help! We have to make sure their own cash does not victimize the taxpayers paying. Like the college graduates with educational loans who cannot get decent jobs. Most of those loans have to be vacated for decent government jobs, or null and voided for breach of contracts, because the unconstitutionally forced-terms have been altered so many time, at pleasure of politicians. If the money vaporizes like the TARP money, some ones will have to be prosecuted, for their shenanigans, but it should not come out of the student pockets at punitive flex rates and harsher loan terms.

Governance

Good governments need to aim their protections and their generosities at their people not at their Executives and CEOs. A 20-25 years old macro-tax policy of keeping real income low disproportionally is a chronic and delayed disaster, having board of trusties and CEO pay Committees without adequate representation from shareholders and workers remain as national follies. The same PR-media discovers the shareholders and workers at blame-time, at pay-time they sell, their souls cheap at cooperate head offices. Governments can establish a control for CEO-pay performance within a free market bands, tied to national and workers' average income index. A 10-year stock-holding performance period, and five to ten years claw backs, or even an emergency cap will dislodge systemic corruptions and dishonesties. If senators are unable to do work, remind them at election time to pass the claw back rule and CEO-pay band-controls. That labor and shareholders have to be placed on the trust-boards and executive-pay committees. They have to mandate shareholders-say in major cooperate-decisions. These have past theoretical and rhetorical phases in the electronic age, and may have to be adopted experimentally or permanently. These cannot be left to inner organizational bulling and, mismanagement. They should have been added to the $700 billion stabilization give away, and watch the outlays as hungry hawks. Ask them to add these rules to the next interim $300,000,000 stimuli-checks they have to send you, before the system starts up again. They can mail you the one million dollar check, or pay you what is left after paying the individuals' mortgage, education loans, health plan bills, credit card loans, and auto loans. Either way, you would have save them $600+ billion dollars and all those emergency socializations to come.

What Remedies

Post-crash, USA 5-7 week's long response is unintentionally too lethargic in these kinds of markets. It indulges on forbearances of the "we the people" and public trust. That would work in normal times. These are not normal times. A Market holiday will allow for appropriate adjustment time, if we cannot rationally match buys and sells. Any time California or New York prime real estates are called "toxic" sites-unseen by offending parties normal does not cover it. It matters very little, if representatives or executive suits have done it. What are the solutions now? Who will be punished? When are the solutions enacted? When will they become effective? Who will do the quality control after studies? Now, we are in the age of electronic, instant decision, which can cost you a fortune. You must allow the old age machinery to kick in, before you can realistically evaluate the result of an action. Beside, some indices can be way off, Hurricanes-unemployment versus longer-term trends. Post hurricane employment can also kick in on the other sides. So, chill for a minute dudes! Ease up people on your "sky is falling screams!" Business production is a process. Capital in all kinds of disasters unlike human-life will be replaced. Politic is also old machinery, it will take time and then they over react! Nothing is wrong with most American businesses, after bad executives are shoed out. Not all of them depend on bank loans, subprime, outside credits or have bad executives. Most of them have billions of cash on hand, and steady revenues, if you buy from them. They are not the problems in the panicky markets you have made them. Your level of panic and fear belatedly causes more problems! There are economic macro-micro-and technological tools for most known issues. However, none of them will work, if panicky people stampede themselves into more poverty, and another cascades down. Unless, the family-budgets have zeroed-out again, around the holidays. It is impossible to put lipstick on the bulls in a stampede.

Good, Bad, and Ugly Advice

The hacks are advising you to sell low and be safe. They will charge you and tell you to buy high later. Remember, they will turn around and buy the good stocks, before they tell you to buy back in. It is like Gold salespersons selling it as a safety-buy! They will tell you to buy gold at $2000, and when the market turns, they will sell gold at $1700, and buy stock at 10,000 DJ. Then, when the cycles turn, you will have to sell gold at $300 again, and buy the DJ at $15000, and pay them both ways. One hopes, that public enlightenment is divined by osmosis, after they have down this a few time, people can analyze those bad idea. What is that saying: about "fooling some of the unfortunate people all of time." So do not be fooled, again! Cash out, out of stocks to your comfort-levels at the euphoric high-peaks, otherwise hang-on for the very bumpy rides, and buy in at the gut-wrenching troughs. Keep a percentage of your cash for stock only 10-20 percent in bad time, and keep a level head if you have "invested" in good stocks, unless you bought wrong as a "day" trader and need to get out. Day-traders will do that and take a tax deduction anyway. If you really believe, there is no value in American industries. There is nothing logical anyone can tell you. So, why are you in the stocks? If you think they have adopted bad policies or bad laws, and they have waved off their constitution, and magna carte, and they have turned self-destructively anti immigrants, then those policies are flex, and can be changed in more secure times, with elections. That is the link between true-democracies and truly free markets. Vote and demand it, and vote again and kick them out, above all put in term limits. The paper capital vaporizes by the distrust and the critical-dishonesties. You add questionable packaging of credit-swaps, derivatives, and complex sub-primes, and soft regulatory institutions, on the real estate bubble, and cut out the demand by anti-immigration, and high decibel intrusions in banking and privacy, turn up volume of confiscatory legalism, anti-workers' crusaders. It would be a surprise, if we do not have multiple capital-market crashes, like now. The real estate capital will be re-injected back by temporal-capital values and investments, global capital and labor mobility, or government intervention and capital-swaps with time lag. Nevertheless, there has to be substantial honest changes. In addition, there has to be sustainable real aggregate demands, from new jobs.

Economics

Now, we live in interesting economic time. Forget real free market economic for the short and med term economic time span. You have to keep a theoretical free market model in mind, so that the solutions will not permanently set to the self-destructive path. That will take self-interest, technological innovation and invention, and production motivation out of the system permanently. The first step was the depression proofing of the banking system that was done. The devils remain in the details, paying for banking system crashes is not wise, Government needs to grab the so-called toxic assets and hang on to them short term. The next step, as essential again, is the immediate term tech-injections, job-creations, or checks, but do not wait forever to make up your mind. Without this step, all next steps are invalid. We will remain in the immediate term until next spring 2009, 2012, or longer. The medium and long term come in as dynamics and sustainability issues of the model. In the longer-term phase, free-market will be fully functional and deterministic to the economy in four to ten years out. Unless the infrastructure silver bullets cover all incidences, it will fail. In addition, government will cash out their stocks and sell out their toxic assets (houses). Everything else and all of these assets have to be put on the you-tube, internet, with full transparency, as soon as, we the people have them, and they will be sold out with a lag to open bids. HUD, United State Department of Housing and Urban development, a division of federal government has done these for a few decades successfully.

Legislative Technological Injections

New rules, naked short-sellers, hedge-fund-take downs for positioning and fee-pay links, destructive international capital-flight, flash-capitals market moves and phantoms cyber electronic moves and crashes (and capital and labor fear-immobility require established uniformed modifications (trust, appropriate supportive immigration regulations, and cyber security firewalls), not to halt total-mobility, but to discourage profiteering from the induced positioning, and reduce immobility damages. It is nominally a better financial free-market solution, to take two-minutes to two-hour stop-market times, or stop-sell-limits on amounts and number of stocks over $250,000 or

2500 shares at a time, after 10 percent price crash, or new uptick rules. A globally coordinated market-holiday for the adoption of such laws can slow damages of rash-fear based decisions. Adjusting to more cash-margin ratios is better than freezing credit activity totally. That will be more toxic. A market-holiday instead of bank holiday can help the governments to activate all or most of the tools, and encourage major institutional to match their buy-sell. Totally banning this or that transaction, or settling for a 29-crash to clear the markets, will only clean out our packets! Finding economic free market solutions to repair the post panic-damages is priceless.

Fiscal Economics

Macroeconomic policy has been simplified to monetary-policy-only at our economic peril. Dysfunctional Legislators have codified it as well. The error has been magnified by monetization and fed-functionality to back policy-makers, as the only solution. If the cycles turn, then everyone will announce victory and move on to better pastures. The jingoistic-success short of the old-nihilistic Hooversim has added to their potency and longevity, that is an applauded accomplishment for monetarism. The old-nihilistic Hooverists and cooperate-political lobbies, all in favor of tax-breaks for cooperation and billionaires, have hijacked fiscal policy for decades. Thick as thieves, no new jobs, same old low wage mantra, and collusions have sustained them well. Sadly, we have ignored the harshest lesson of the 1920s. This macro-economic theoretical law, "the real disposable wage-income asserts the 75 percent force multiplier on the demand side pull or push on the whole economy," they are consequential movements. Dilution of indices by the 1 percent upper income brackets, and cooperate-executive-pays will not uniformly spread, or pacify the upward mal-redistributions of real income and wealth concentration, hence, a demand-side crash has been caused, and it is here now, it will remain until major policy changes are shaped, passed, and actually carried out. The small scales FDR administration model, the infrastructure-job-creation model with small marginal real-income injections in the economy prolonged the post-depression recovery phase two to three decades. The enhancements and expansions made it a functional, eventually. That explanation had eluded most monetary-lobbyists, more supply side fanatics, and fundamentalists. Federal Reserve often is wedged between mandates, and economic reality requiring legislative fiscal (tax-Job creation) strategies, or lately, the dysfunctional dualism.

Since this last spring market drop, the stimuli-check expectation sustained the economy until the October Market Crash of 2008, in 2001 it worked faster and better because consumers had more savings, or a better margin to borrow and spend. The monetarists and other institutions have had since 1987, then 1990s, to repair the damage to the market trust accumulated around the derivatives, sub-primes, and credit-swaps, and all monetary-market capital instruments. The monetarists have had since 1975 when late Milton Friedman days to shift the wealth-housing link from credit (home-equity, credit cards, students' loans) spending to wage-job real disposable income sources. A monetary solution alone will elongate the economic malaise for decade or two. Yet, there will be the 3-9-11 years' interim cyclical downturns or crashes. (Short kitchen cycles to Kondratieff longer cycles,) we used to call them recessions. Expectation forces also work up to the certain time, when the investors feel it has become a rigged game.

Climax and Resolutions

Major spending PAYGO, modification of certain out of control spending in forever wars, long-wars, and other southern strategy solutions, and military-industrial-politico complex gravy-trains will take place, after short and midterm remedies stabilize our current predicaments.

A more truthful cooperate ethic-regulations with punitive teeth and jail terms will replace do what you want cooperate regimes. Substantial job-creation strategies, educational retaining for designated-jobs cannot be shirked-off without political costs. A unified social security-military-political retirement-benefit fund for all Americans should not be ignored anymore.

A health care system including Medicare, catastrophic care and childcare and preventive health visits, and prenatal and geriatric cares as a base-unified-transferable core-health-plan cannot be ignored. All other exotica and add-ons can still be under private insurances. What has been passed on to the consumers as health-insurance premiums, beyond and above the minimum cost of an individual universal coverage, is a major tax on their disposable income. Blaming the poor, middle class, immigrants, jobless, employed poor, fear mongering, and warmongering are part of those self-destructive nihilistic southern strategies we need to discard, you cannot use them and hide anymore, especially in political-ads.

Fairness doctrine is an essential addition the forth stool of the three branches of USA government. With or without the shield act it will guarantee some expanded force to the free media and first amendment essentials for cleaner governance. The younger generations can remind the outdated strategists that intellectually, economically, morally, and ethically they take a more inclusive and constructive view of the global future. These basic three prongs-solutions (in immediate, medium, and long-term time-span) will pull the USA and global economy out their current conundrums on solid long-term growth pass. People have more optimistic, common, and familial hopes and likes, more than antagonistic dislikes. Their leaders need to mimic their better cultural qualities.

States' Benz-Republicanism, Legal Immigration Fiasco

The deeper roots of regional “declinism" and "Imperial Overstretch," require longer analytical studies. The National Science Foundation budget should be expanded to deal with these kinds of economic problem. There have been books written that go back to the book "Fall of Rome." Nevertheless, the rest of nations or humanity does not need to go down with these socio-pathological down turns.[2]

Nationally we have been down that dark and gloomy nightmarish path to no-good. Dred Scott biography and the Supreme Court moment did not enlighten us.[34] Even Lincoln speech did not move us.[5] So Civil war came and went. We did not get educated as a nation. The thirteen-amendment was added, they bested the law, 14th amendment, and they want to abolish it, now. Hypoes Corpus, they restrict it, bent it, want to abolish it, why?

The Peonage laws came, some played it and went right back, to neo-slavery for profit.[6] The Gandhi, and the civil law, Dr. Martin Luther king Jr. Came, justice Thurgood Marshall came, Nelson Mandela's experiences are still fresher in our mind, and he is here, volumes of commerce clauses have been added, federal separations of duties were adopted early on, and they have been expanded. So here, we are again, we want taxpayers' money to make state malleable laws for their own interests.[7]

> "The neoslavery system exploited legal loopholes and federal policies which discouraged prosecution of whites for continuing to hold black workers against their wills. As it poured millions of dollars into southern government treasuries, the new slavery also became a key instrument in the terrorization of African Americans seeking full participation in the U.S. political system."

Moreover, Arizona wants to establish a legal precedence in reaffirming the mentality of Oklahoma Federal building perpetrators' cultural stump, and anti-multiculturalism of global terrorists on Immigrations laws.

Death of Immigrants in Detention

In some mindset take the word black out, and replaced it with immigrant, or illegals, we want to go right back into the cultural wilderness, again.[8] In the post 9-11 hysteria and fear, some new agencies were formulated. The legal quality control, corrective laws, or shut off mechanisms exploded taxpayers cost, and imposed on civil right laws extensively.

The atmospherics have at best had the rotten apple syndrome influences on other agencies.[9] There are immediate issues with such quick fix up agencies,

1. Unfamiliar agencies make public observation difficult.
2. There is little regulatory enforcement developed, in misuse of weapons, bad techniques.
3. Inadequate weapon training and self-control are readily adopted.

4. Cases go unseen, or unprosecuted, thus encourage criminal conducts.
5. In this example, a video is recording a groups' criminal misconduct, the immigrant in handcuff and leg chains is dead, the brutality and hate crime continues.

Unfortunately, such criminal or at best marginal behaviors and misbehaviors crave protective cloaks, for obvious reasons, they fear true public opinions, and backlash.[10] An important way to measure dishonest anti-immigrant straw media polls is to pick different internet reports with videos, then tally responses of the first ten, or the first hundred. You will get a percentage result, in this video-case of beating death above 80 percent agree that a violent-group- crime is brutally and criminally happening, like in GETMO, or Abo Ghribe-Iraq, but this is in USA-land, and there are accumulated data of death of immigrants in detentions. Moreover, increasing signs of official lethargy in hiding and none prosecution of the crimes associated with those deaths. In face of discovery of the deceits, and fear potential legal actions, if their conducts are discovered, they seek legalisms.[11] They seek protective cover, by legalistic maneuvering all the way to the Supreme Court. Here there are a few more cases, when officials state their intentions.[12]

These gets uglier and ethically incomprehensible, if one can read simple English, honestly, and has some minimal ethical and moral requirements, barely that over a rotten cumquat (or a rancid broccoli),

> "Two of those deaths had occurred in Arizona, in 2004 and 2007, at the Eloy Detention Center, run by the Corrections Corporation of America. Eloy had nine known fatalities — more than any other immigration jail under contract to the federal government. But Immigration and Customs Enforcement was still secretive. When a reporter for The Arizona Republic asked about the circumstances of those deaths, an agency spokesman told him the records were unavailable.[13]

As more outer onion-skins comes off daily, more of links between the certain political party and the neo Nazi, skin head, neo fascists, hate movements, race groups, and dangerously subversive movements are discovered.

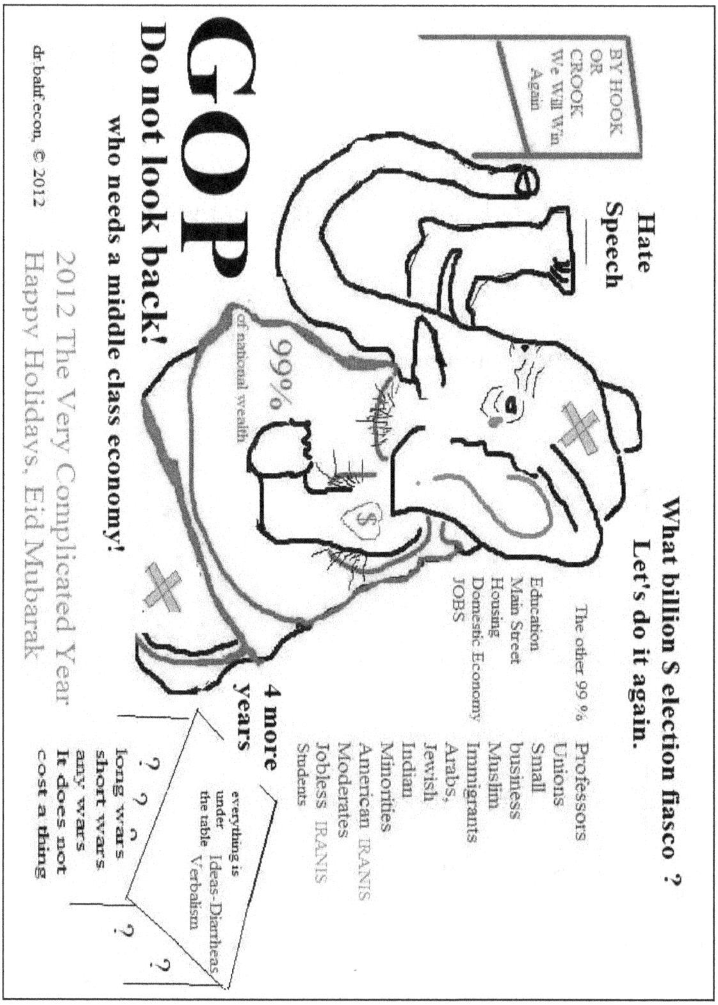

Copycat States in Denial

Some of these states had gathered the required knowledge, and advice to try economic growth through economic investments by different global industries, obviously from exogenous and foreign economists, educators, and scholars. Some of their enlightened governors preach the overt merits of technological injection in reviving their economies. So much so, that Toyota, Honda and Mercedes Benz Republicans have been trumpeting their legislative success from these borrowed but transient events into a perceived expertise over the Federal Immigration laws.[14] That is when the fatal reductionism in logic takes shape. Here is another recent fiasco among others that oozes out of their legal remedies.[15] For more specific and the names, refer to the article.[16] After giving tax breaks to cooperation to locate in economically backward states, their police incarcerates an executive, as an illegal, because he did not have papers on him.

Unfortunately, the emotional and superficial appeals have buffaloed some national political intellects to go along with their xenophobic myopic backwater views of modernity in today's complex global economic conditions, regardless of the consequential ruinous economics results in states after states. It is a viral ideologues' fundamentalism.

That is not rational, regardless of the window dressing, when they run out of logical reasons to fix the immigration law (comprehensive immigration law, or expanded dream-acts).[17] They take off and join the lemmings off the ledge of reason into the ice-cold blue ocean of xenophobia. Let us hope the Supreme Court will divine supreme reasons that the constitutionalists' separation of powers and duties were not bunk, as certain states jeer on with the ideologues' Band-Aids, while the patient dies of the festering old wounds. They can wisely choose to bleed the patient to death, while we watch whichever comes first, the overall cure or the economic bloodlettings. Instead of harvesting and sharing the fortunate result of their received bounties, they completely misinterpret their own jingoism and triumphalism into anti-immigration dystopias, or the new comical self-deportation model. The famed Stalinist version of "ends justify the means" should not explain The American immigration laws. Even worst, the nationalist socialist party of Germany (Adolf Hitler's model) following the race purity-logic of early anti-immigration laws' verbiages of USA representatives should not be repeated domestically.[18] Worst yet, a string of xenophobic bigoted states fallowed these idiocies off the proverbial lemming ledge, ledges or sites unstudied, or unseen. Whether, we are talking the dollars amount of $23,000 per each deportation, or the normal $ 53,000 per annum per each incarceration (even in the self-leaking ice creams of the private chains), the government revenues of employed workers are also cut out. Therefore, if they really succeed and vacate everyone, apply the neo-fascists' pipe dreams of self-deportation, or scare them under ground, into tax free black market economies, (like where all of the big businesses, have gone legally, this side of Swiss and Cayman islands bank accounts). The macroeconomic will be victimized, again.

This economy can ill afford to lose 1.5 trillion dollars, \$23-\$53 billions, and damages in farm, fruit and vegetable, meat, agriculture industries, hospitality, and tourists' industries. The jobless American cannot afford multiple additional job losses in cascading chain reactions. There are no ways to goose-step an upside out of these negative externalities and economically cascading negative externalities, which was unleashed by the 1996-immigration law, and its slow macroeconomic consequences from California, South, and South East.

Therefore, instead, this frozen turkey from heavens hits them square on their thick silly noggins.[19] Given the regional histrionics, it is not quite a surprised to everyone.

> "The former Nazi and Ku Klux Klan Grand Wizard ran for Governor of Louisiana in a campaign based on an open appeal to white people who feel they are being cheated of their American birthright by blacks, immigrants, liberals, New Yorkers, and similar bogeys."

There have been many voices, studies, and attempts to reintroduce rationality in this melee of xenophobic bigotry, rational (comprehensive, dream acts) immigration laws have failed to penetrate the emotionalism, and preconceived fake statistics, over paid bloviated radio and TV spinners. Yet, as moth to the flames, in these dark economic nights, their natures flames them ruinously.

They keep raising the risk, insecurities, and mistrust premiums on international investments in their regions. They have to give more tax breaks, and front loans in billions out of a declining taxpayer's bases, and tax revenues to induce such investments. Then, with straight face, they exaggerate health costs of a few immigrant children in the emergency rooms, pens, and pencils and education costs, which are free in most other industrial nations. Department of justice, legal action against discriminatory and constitutional actions is another helping hand, which they will bite vociferously.[20]

> "Dozens of House Democrats have joined the Obama administration's lawsuit against Alabama's contentious new law against illegal immigrants."

This must be the week for idiotic woops, and self-dealing and adulations among the chosen elitists, and the under-taxed classes. The bogus claims that unemployment, they mean natives' underemployment of 9-19 percent, is caused by foreign influences especially illegal immigration. This is an emotional release value for seriously under educated, alienated, jobless and discarded portion of population, with unemployment of 25 percent and higher.[21] These follow a series of wrongheaded policies, and adopted policies hostile to human and capital market movements.

The multiyear extreme risk and uncertainty are injected into the market under false flags, and emotional waves of ignorant responses, to some real, but mostly imagined fears and bogymen others, under security guises.[22] These trends are more pronounced in under developed and riskier economic regions, which physical capitals, financial capitals, and smarter human capital often avoid.

Political parties win office by demagogical sunshine patriotism and enact such policies, fail miserably their states. Because these xenophobic and bigoted and misogynistic, and sexist, racists' politics in modern post news-cooperation controlled multimedia exposures fail to ameliorate economic conditions, particularly smaller regional or state economies. These regional economies often invite double dip recessions. They can stay in multiyear stagflations instead of normal recovery in counter cycles. In the age of multimedia alertness, their populations are alerted instantly to these shortcomings, and political office intrigues. We will see quicker recalls in democratic regions, and harsher democratic remedies in non-democratic regions.

Globally, Euro-neo-fascism spreads among youth, and extremists' parties feasting on bad economic reasons and deteriorating economic condition, which war deficit financing has worsened.[23] Instead of the prescribed domestic or regional investment-deficits financing, which should improve economic conditions by job creations? The spread of the former viral imbecilities shows no sign of intellectual subsiding. Those are the best reasons for probable euro-economic backslide into the double dip. Thanks all the immortals up there working double time to save the middle class, workers, immigrants, educators, students, and some police and fire persons from these moronic self-destructive nihilistic imbeciles.[24]

Since they have are making legislative claims in other areas of pollution on EPA, on Drugs and FAA,

Fracking and Energy department, it is high time for the voters to pay closer attention to these miss-behaving for reelection campaign money. Term Limit, next to recalls has such a nice freedom ring to it. Even the smarter educated republicans are calling for it.[25] They need to be welcomed to the politics as much as the establishment would like to expunge them.

Peace, Technological Injections, Economics

The gestalt of the foreign policy toward Islamic nations, the 1.6 million Oma, cannot be a Hopson choice between psychosis and SCHADENFREUDE, to propagate dystopian dictatorships. It has to be based on foundational of diplomacy and truth telling, potentially contradictory matters. Otherwise, extremists, abstractionists, war profiteers, and destructionists will drive our policy off and away from the progressive roads. The people of these nations like our middle classes have to see a positive drive and an agenda of peace and prosperity, a constructionists' plan ahead for themselves and their children. Constantly, threatening them, mounting difficulties for paid, illegal, and induced casus belli, burdensome regulatory abuses, after what they have gone through will have contrary unpleasant results. It will devitalize moderation among the dwindling intellectual middle classes, and grow the hordes of energetic Dead Enders contrary to stated national and global security needs, and their own humane needs.

How can people ignore the war *putz*? That is necessary and sufficient conditions for a sustained successful pre-election economic-recovery to continue, even after the election.[26] At the tail end of a week, which war hysteria for another preemptive-intrusion is induced by the war parties of intellectually and financially bankrupted. We need a refresher course of historical rebooting.

HAPPY NUROOZ-2012 message to Iran out of the Israeli mouth in United States White House is a new preemptive war, words put there a few week back by visiting Neocon representatives.[27] USA Jobless of the recent economic tornado and Tornado Alley victims (Kentucky, and South) need USA attention and resources. The post Sandy storm of North East victims of New Jersey and New York outer islands also need substantial rebuilding aids. Remember last president was looking out of the airplane window, after hurricane Katrina. These regions contribute substantially to the government and private capital revenues of nation.

Likud and the GOP-PACs (political action committees) have a different agenda.[28] It is not, to fix domestic American economy. It is to send cash overseas, into the untraced hinterlands, and tax heaven bank accounts. Moreover, it is just to get a minority President out of the White House. Vegas money, Arizona, Florida, C-PACs & I-PACs (AIPAC) and other Israeli PACs' money, and three yearlong republicans' rhetoric are on this, too, against the best interest and national security vitals of United States, and the exposed soldiers on the ground.[29]

Their media manipulators' stakes are in this hook or crook as well.[30] Their multiple election losses have not informed, educated, or deter their misinformed logic.

They have fueled the flames of holy wars, blew every dog vessels of hate by design to set off a war on Islam, while praying for overreactions and backlash, from both Islamic, and Christian nations. Some self-proclaimed pastor threatens and then burns the book of Islam, Quran (Qhuran). Everyone gets the connotations that an idiot is self-promoting his cultish belief, except villagers in the hinterlands, which are as backward and fanatical as some southern sub-theologians are.[31] However, the villagers, who do not have law-degrees from USA religious degree-mill colleges, were not initially burning Bibles or Torah. Another band of GI-Jackasses try to show how not to be honorable soldiers, and abuse dead victims, except, they endanger and bad name real honorable soldiers, and their own national security interests, against their own codes of conduct, and against severe admonitions of their civilian and military commands. Then, we have more of the same.[32] At tail end of Vietnam War, as such, things were divulged, and some were discovered, all military and veterans paid the price in negative backlashes, and later low employment. In ignorance, they bit the capable hands, which are trying to navigate them. Many political leaders have been pleading your cases, as you are quickly undoing them. While presidents, senators, congressional representatives, and well-wishers will contribute to your success, very little they can do out of office, to stop the consequences of the silence over-reactions, of silence majority.[33] As more criminal-conducts, murderous-rampages go under punished over here, the worst of the social reactions and cultural shock will be over there.

However, there are the other latent quiet social reactions. There will be much less tolerance for public misbehaviors and perceived misconducts back home. Big businesses (not hippies or just liberals) will employ them less over here, and let them go much faster, at any sign of exaggerated misconducts, use healthcare issues, or health care laws as an excuse to withhold employment. Some big businesses like the Vietnam era, will avoid the perceived risks all together, or wait for the quiet hours to do it later. The nation the patriotic Americans, the honorable solders, their families, have been around these merry-go-around during the Vietnam War, and post-Vietnam war epochs. They bore the scars, and paid the full price. The bulging unemployed homeless Vietnam vets formed fast, and dissipated unconscionably slowly.

It is an adult world. Yet, the 18-year-old soldiers are the America to ambassadors. They easily forget the multimedia-technological revolution, not always the WikiLeaks, make their living rooms back homes their stage, their judge and jury. Moreover, the lop top global are their constant observers. No other warriors, generals, kings, and presidents survive bad publicities, and instantaneous transparencies of their bad judgments. They need to stay the best faces of bad situations.

So here we are, none conformists and opportunists show up to demand and impose their own tortured national security agenda and other of neocon wars on a USA president, timed to impact domestic American election results. Nevertheless, he is going to be there for four more years. More wars depend, if there are true negotiations, diplomacy, and not SHADENFRUDE. It may be time for reopening of diplomatic Chay khaneh for *tshatshke*, and dispense with international megalomaniac clowns' showboats, their military-political-industrial complexes, their domestic agents, and agendas.

There is the American myth about conflicts stopping at the waters' edge, another myth of diplomacy is that above all do not do harm. We know the myths are not true, now. So, the republican dilatants transubstantiated themselves in the presidency, at the behest of Likud-radicals, to abnegate United States foreign policy to a third nation, an act they would readily portray as treasonous and treacherous by others, by sleeper cells. Yet, here we are looking at it in suspended belief, hoping the republican sleeper cells wake themselves up. What bunch of *Mavens.* Was it to abolish bipartisan presidential requests and decrees to allow a two states solution, was it to postpone giving back occupied territory to Syria, to reduce tensions, or ameliorate global conflicts. Were these the father and grandfathers of 9-11spymasters showing us how they mastered the manipulation art of people emotions, to subvert and delete constitutional protections, and transpose blames to their victims? They blame everything and everybody for what they regularly cause, like the Nazism they have mimicked, and the other real Holocausts they are duplicating on occupied people inside and outside their own borders, and the Stalinism they wish to impose on

American people one intrusive law after another, after each backlash and reaction to their own misdeeds. Was it to push the United States to transude from requesting moderation, to stop invasion from the north again, to request their occupied territories back. They have promised it since the Egypt accords, like an over the hill flirty belly dancers? If Mr. Begin was scared from enforcing settlement bans, he would have not initiated the Egyptian Peace accords. The chief terrorist during Ingrum years and father of Likud political party, later he won over his fear and loathing for peace. Likud must find a bigger braver prime minster like Begin and to push peace on their outliers, since their neighborhood has changed, instead of pushing the global war in fear.[34] There are no signs of such backbone in their present Likud leadership. It takes *chutzpah* to seek *shalom*. He gave into the jackals of war visiting him a week before his embracive visit to White House empty handed. *Oy gevalt*, only a *mashugana schmuck* listens to those old wars' *putz and* their *shticks*, they are mouthing and jeering war generals now, they said we should listen to them before. They also visited Afghanistan, and we have an evolving catastrophe there too, Americans domestic economy awaits the declarative win, and the departure. Was it just to bully another friendly supportive nation to engage in another ill-conceived unfunded nihilistic neocon war, which cost everyone and kneecaps American economy and global interests, and yields another nothing? Was it just to hide criminality of intend and deeds, to further fuel the flames of intolerance and cross cultural hate, so a small gesture of compliance long requested by United States Presidents of both parties are squashed, again? We hope the next visitors are not here to request reinvading Normandy, or our friends in Poland. Her majesties public servants show more wisdom than that.

SCHADENFREUDE, it is an obstructionists' strategy, mixed with enjoyment obtained from the troubles of others. It has garnished substantial amount of negative externalities nationally, and even more, internationally. It is most destructive when pathological, or psychotic aspects of militarism, (vengeance, false patriotism, war profiteering, medals and rank-seekers, and multiple dippers) dominate national psychics, and edge out national security, national and international stated principles, goals, and diplomacy.

President Eisenhower understood the influences of long war psychosis on national and international economies. It very often follows multiple mission creeps. It is also cascading. It is global, and it will cost taxpayers fortunes in trillions, beyond $4-6 per gallon of gas. This is much bigger than ZEITGEST riptides pulling the economy under.[35] ZEITGEST a 1769-1835 German word is defined as moral, intellectual, and cultural climate of an era. It can apply to a nation or group of nations sharing these characteristics. However, a fuller understanding come from its Latin source "GENIUS SECULI" Genius "guardian spirit, attendant spirit", and saeculi "of the ages" portray a more comprehensive meaning. Make sure whoever starts the next neocon war, pays for it, and for Syria, Libya, Egypt, Iraq, Afghanistan, Pakistan, Yemen, Sudan, Lebanon, and the two states Palestinians. If we reached a national and international consensus that Afghanistan or Pakistan neglected, isolated, and abandoned created existential insecurities, there are few logical foundations to add to it or multiple the risks-factors by tenfold. American historical amnesia forgets the Marshall plan and euro-Japanese economic rebuilds, after the President Eisenhower 4 year World War Two victory. Eleven years of murky Middle East invasions, and American multiple down turns, leave questionable resources for domestic rebuilds, let alone another economic Marshals plan to finish the job in Middle East or Africa.

These could morph into religious wars, by hate fumes and SCHADENFREUDE. Before the austerity <bologna> baloney got too thick, republicans wanted to underfund social security, Medicare, education funding, student loans, they went after teachers and professors pay raises, unions, legal immigrant, women health issues, and legacy pensions to reduce the deficit. They should raise the one presenters' taxes 5 percent, and establish an alternative cooperate minimum tax for the tax avoidance INCs, to help pay for the other two wars, they started. They forget they did this from social security lockbox, but they swiftly transferred the revenue into tax breaks for the highest incomes. Fresh from the cultural wars on women health, on minorities, on legal immigrants, what kind of honey wagon came in town, which helped Washington to misplace their senses, and they are so self-lubricating with holy ointments for two new wars? They were not willing or able to do domestic business, small business, infrastructures, job creation for last three years. What did the Israeli defense-political-industrial complex promised them may be the rest of us, the American tax payers, the middle class can get some of that promised holy-ointments, to get them to work for the free healthcare, and lifelong-pensions, and multiple-dipping they get. God knows the middle class has paid for it. They are paid when they do not do their jobs. They exempt themselves of the nastiest they pass as laws for the middle class. They get free healthcare and pensions for life.

Now, all that clowning around about bombing people, and letting go the choirboys and underage pages for holy wars will cost treasures and blood, none of which the one-percent are willing to pay for.[36] These Middle East countries will require one trillion each without a war, which are about ten trillions in the longer run. They can easily sink into the failed state economies, even without another war. We need the true technological injections, the bifurcated political institutions of democracies, and long-term development-plans for these nations, and the economic sustainability of these allegedly budding democracies, after we repair American economy, to reduce massive debts over time, or a new Afro-Middle east Marshall Plan.

What we do not need are the megalomaniacs to push another war on us, reroute our resources, the Americans' taxpayers' funds from domestic capital formations and job creation from our cities and economies to Israeli Likud's land grabs, and murderous imploding plots for odiously portraits of leaders, or phantom theologies. These Israeli allies seem to have mastered the political knack for one term of government service and grab all you can, and a one-way ticket to jail, a political Madoff-ism with the American taxpayers' money, regardless of the additional cost to the Jews, *goyem,* and gentiles globally. Let assume the neocons, were not the fifth column, they were not deep in pentagon from Israel, adumbrating their Likud plans. They were not in the Bush's White House pushing the Iraq war, even before the 9-11. They were not contorting the weapon of mass deceptions, then and now. So, who were their masters, pushing for long wars, and why? Why are they playing the same games, the same patterns, now? Why did the USA economy tanked, and minority unemployment spiked into teens and twenties, and now it is joined by the veterans' unemployment indices? What is the verbosity over 1966 borders, instead of 1955 borders all Palestinians' lands, and the UN determined border? Why are these war criminals calling USA presidents anti-Semites, and USA Generals weaklings.[37] Are these to undermined their diplomacy abroad, and goat them into nihilistic wars domestically?[38] They did want a regime change for a better self-dealing climate, regardless of USA interests.

Prime minster and defense minister Yitzhak Rabin 1922–1995 was assassinated by right wing Likud. He was boastfully shot in the head, in bright daylight. Right-wing conservatives and Likud leaders, who perceived the Oslo peace process as forfeiture of the occupied territories (from Palestinians and Syrians, Jordanians and Egyptians), disparaged him personally, before they killed him, and stopped another peace process.

Mr. Bull, a Canadian engineer was shot five times in his head, before the Iraq war, now those war-crime-syndromes are in full epidemics. Of course, they are here to find a soft touch to hide behind another war, and trillions in loose change to pay for it. However, who is ready for that donkeys' tail. The Southern pastors, the republicans, our treasury department can they write the checks. Let us ask them for their share of the trillions in new taxes, now.

A USA Chief economist was dismissed, because he said the Iraq-war might cost a few billions. A USA secretary of treasury left his job in opposition. All republicans even dismissed a few generals. Now 4 to 7 trillion dollars later, austerity postures go out of the window for the same fearful ideologues with blood lust. That is why you are here, you want company as you descent into the Dante's seventh level of Hell for murderous Holocaust on Palestinian people and landowners. The two state settlements-solutions, forgotten. Palestinian people, they only know terrorists, Islamist Jihadists, no such landowners exists.[39] They have silenced them all. Beside another two little wars, you want the American voters, taxpayers to squeeze you in the White House, like a rich man through the eye of a needle. Where is the irrelevant and discarded UN in all of this nonsense? They playing *schlemiel,* they vanished with the Palestinian landowners, Iraqi war victims, and the disposes-others. Where did they these shameless dissevers of Baghdad, hide their evidences of mass destruction of Iraqi nuclear developments. Why are they allowed back, for the highest bidders, with the same shell games? Nevertheless, they will show up, to claim financial purses, to accommodate and read capitulation statements over the Neo-Holocausts, starving children, and the damaged and vanquished economies of third world, and radiated dispossessed persons, the Islamic-Oma.

Well, *mazltof*, good luck with that, HAPPY SPRING and PEACE dudes. Iranian people cannot trust you with their national self-defense, and security under any old or new flags, or their future energy supplies. Neither did the Israeli people, what is great for goose, is fantastic for the ganders. You robbed the Iranian people and their democracy after the AJAX 1950s, displaced their democratic parliament with dictatorship to steal the oil money that was the 1950 solution.

The imposed Iraq-Iran war did not come without your handshakes of approval, what did the blood lust got

Iranians, Americans, Kurds, Iraqis, Arabs, Muslims, Jews. Now, the same oil cooperation- plutocrats are financing and manipulating your election-campaigns domestically. Under the Shah you wanted, and actually carried over there nuclear weapons, establish medical radioactive facilities. Now, it is an existential threat to the future resource robbery, if they get nuclear energy. What guarantee we have from the fronted foundations, American or International foundations, or the bifurcated people houses of dysfunctional-ill reputes, corrupted media models that any of our rights, any of human rights, or financial rights, or even laws will be respected? All the damages, which have amassed to us and Iranian people since 1950s for the oil industry oligopolies, the monopoly oil contracts, the white revolution and the shah's land grabs from small landowners, have never been repaid.[40] May the love of a real Allah, a true God comfort you with your descents? You must know by now, it is mostly if not totally self-inflected. Ben Laden is dead, great, however, the BenLadenism shall not parish with him, and the infiltrated and corrupted military-security-political-industrial complex will not let a profitable self-leaking ice cream parish. That is the only angle left on the diminishing middle-class taxing revenues, and self-curtailing recursive war-economy.

The USA economy recovery could be functioning on the fumes of Santa's hot air. Just do not lose your economic marbles, in your SCHADENFREUDE repeatedly. Focus on domestic job creation, infrastructure, and repertory economic recovery.

Cheer up, the republicans can still win, and start and lose another two wars, which we all have to pay for, against their own better and older wisdoms.[41] On the other hand, they may fail and disband as a hate group, after they denigrate and declare wars on elderly, educators and students, the middle class, legal immigrants, black and Asian Americans, American Indians and other minorities, and the women voters, and the increasing veterans and veteran-minorities, and generally unemployed millions. Sorry, for the *shmaltzy shmooze*, and retour of history, but what is a little *FAI*, among friends. It is time for goyems' retentions of hard lessons, all the way to November election and beyond. Thus Americans embrace Trumpism.

When time has aged you,
And your youth have fled

Not even a mystic can divine you,
The mysteries of ages;

When beauty has passed, and grace is in your head,
And compassion has fled.

Not even a mystic can divine you,
The mysteries of life;

Let stay human in your heart,
And let the nescience heads flee

Then even a mystic can divine you,
The mysteries of love;

Let knowledge find you,
And let ignorance flee

Then, an educated mystic will divine you,
The mysteries of lives

Financial Boycott of Dirty Dozens

Anti-Immigration laws seemingly fresh out of Neo-Nazi and white-only-indoctrination camps, with expensive anti-constitutional cool-aids, and many idiots willing to drink it up are here.[42] It is sad and backward. It is retro, but it is here.

Diplomacy and schachtism are not based on, narcissism, psychosis, or SCHADENFREUDE. It has to be an agreed balance of all forces and sides, if we are still talking free enterprise and democratic diplomacy. If the gestalts of some policies are hate of others, despising unions, up ending laws, the constitutional laws, disregards for workers, homeowners, student, middle class, educators (the book leaners) it will become very difficult to pray guidance and good intentions on the nutty radical right. In addition, when they decidedly with their actions, repeatedly shun, any attempts to resolutions or settlement. We have to get the message, in a democracy, or we collectively pay a bigger price for it.

The gestalt of our foreign policy toward Islamic nations cannot be a Hopson choice between psychoses, or SCHADENFREUDE, between our ways is the only way, or war. It has to be based on foundation of diplomacy and truth telling, potentially contradictory ideas in some unethical spheres.

States in United States agreed on certain rules of law under constitutional divisions, the articles of confederation, are all in simple English. That is mostly to avoid the pitfalls of ill mannered, haphazardly undereducated few, which in some states deride the good of the many, and the welfare of whole nation for their own narrowed benefits, without bothering to convince, not just inform, or wag their finger at other states, and statesmen, men and women for their votes. It is one thing to uphold law, as your beacon of light and salvation, however, if you are nullifying a bigger, better, constitutional laws to bash others over the head, you have lost the argument.[43] We regret Justice Holms reworded statement, "and then law is made an ASS" rings true occasionally. Caveat Emptor is an apt warning with Arizona papers-please Law. This is the unmonitored-imploding hate-culture seeking political legitimization. It will have a huge political and economic impact, especially on the election. Now, they are imposing on the Supreme Court to expand and legitimize their extremists' political intends, as a Republican Party movement. So that their Neo-Nazi, Neocons' dream-government can take shape and they can purify American government, academia, and the court, and impose the tyranny of minorities as they define them! We saw that movie with subtitles.

Total financial boycott of Arizona and half of dirty dozen, states' commerce has been called for until certain anti-constitutional laws are modified. Moreover, the newer version of beg thy neighbor policies, which has shifted to xenophobic policies and politics fee, robbery, and kick thy neighbors in these states' dystopian exceptionalism have to stop. The observations have to satisfy all human right, pro civil right, pro humane uses of constitutional laws, all academics, students, all libertarians, and all minorities, and all immigrants and their fellow citizens, and of course some religions and clergies. As long as, they are ratcheting up bad and punitive laws, and teaming up to violate the constitutional, rights of others, the boycotts have to help return the favors.

The anti-constitutional laws have to be punished within the law by all Americans and law-abiding people, nationally and globally.

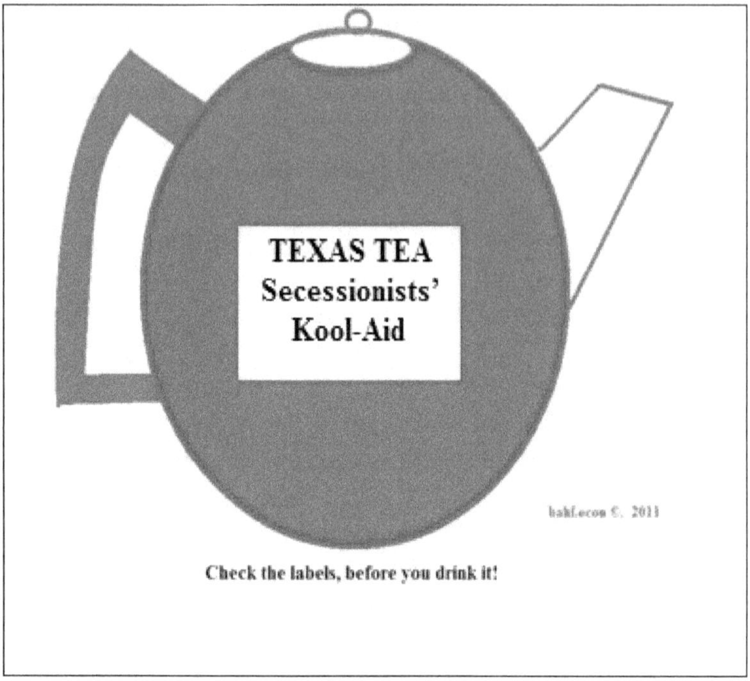

This boycott, as much as it is possible, is against any purchases, visiting, tourism, or supporting anything from Arizona and the copycats bigoted and xenophobic states, unless it comes from a minorities, educational institutions, or Native Americans directly.

The xenophobic, bigoted anti-civil right, anti-immigration republicans, the haters got a victory in Arizona and they aim to metathesize it nationally. This is after years of fighting King's civil right and hotheaded hate talks. This is after they have done their anti-minority southern-strategies in universities, schools, and education to clean it from minorities.

They had their way in Arizona. They did not pass a sensible immigration law. They did not support any immigration laws, they did not streamline or expedite citizenship tracks of legal immigrants here for years, they just added fees, confusions, and overloaded the system to breaking point. That is not their intention to help immigrants, or United States. Instead, they passed a Stalin's communist law as their SS-bodies did in train stations and airports, goose stepping around in Germany. They walk to you and ask for your papers. It feed the insecurity of schoolyard-failed bullies. You look different, show us your paper, or we will put your in our commercialized jails and charge the middle-class taxpayers daily rates for you. You could be immigrants, but as they

have often done it, you can be a child of black, or brown, have a strange name, or be a Native American. You are guilty and subject to police detention, now in zeal of and psychological shocks of post 9-11 overkills, unfortunately, a potential death sentence for some.[44] This is in the global-media age of discoveries that citizens have been falsely accused, jailed, and executed in high numbers. The anti-constitutional profiling laws are on steroids
in Arizona now, later they will be in your states.

We know anything can get in political office these days. Nevertheless, if the fascists do not have self-control with their hates, they have to be confronted in the court of public opinion like their accused. They also need to face the constitution of United States, which they are undoing first, and ask for permission, later. Utah, is one
the latest victims of these idiocy, and rebel raisings. Unfathomably for this State of many decent people, they appear like dressed up moms and pop in their formals,

showing to the cannibals' ball. Moreover, they want to gain positive publicity from this unconstitutional saga.[45] It looks as these lawmakers have stayed in state liquor stores, much too long, against their own good book teachings.

Why are they getting Federal funding, while fighting federal civil laws? A total boycott is the most peaceful civil-disobedient judgments we have against dangerously out of control anti-constitutionalists' secessionists, and haters of our time. Please, use it, to save yourselves. In addition, remind others. Immigrants are the new bugaboo, they use anything to get in your all-American finances, your all-American private phone calls, your American e-mails, and they will lie about it to do so. They were not even looking at a known threat, when he got on a chain of plains. However, they are there to use the news to pass laws against you. They will never run out of bad ideas. Stalin never did, even after he was dead and buried for years. Naked picture scans, groping, later Israeli tactics, like chatting you up before the anal or vaginal probing, and free colonoscopy but not socialized medicine! Or newer naked scans! That is neo-fascism. That is, the other faces of the Neocons-Republicanism.[46] That one, they will deny too.

State lawmakers have approved a sweeping immigration bill intended to change law enforcement efforts in Arizona.[47] There are political aftershocks to such harmful power grab of law. Some of the financial damages were noted above by changing the time line of events.

> PHOENIX (AP) - A sweeping immigration bill intended to ramp up law enforcement efforts in Arizona has been approved by state lawmakers. Perhaps most controversial of all, it requires police to check immigration documents. It was a party line vote with all republicans voting yes and all democrats voting no.
> Sen. Pearce, of Mesa, **(now the object of a successful recall by citizen petition)** has tried for years to get the bill's provisions into law. Immigrants' rights groups who were protesting at the Capitol called it a disgrace."

There are difficulties in enforcement and garnishing local support of the most victimized elements of the discriminated societies.[48] The educated members of the law enforcements' community recognize the heightened danger to them immediately, but to the society incrementally.[49] The injected fear of local law enforcers, will remove sufficient assists and sustainable contacts by all of the community including victims, from the essential and developed tools of appropriate policing in modern times.

Reject Their Failed Ways, Always!

Nothing is worse than some republicans' self-imploding attack-noises lately. For these hate noises to be identified as constructive criticism from loyal opposition is excessively illogical. Even worst have been what southern strategists are doing, that have an elected good black man in front of them in high office, and any kind of flag of jingoistic-patriotism or white-sheets to disguise them.

They go biblical on their own sorry lives, and they want to take the civilizations and the reputation of gentiles and deities, good men and good women of the south, people of all colors and creeds down in the honey well of history with their own sorry selves. We just cannot let them fictionalized the constitution, and join them in this mud volleying with the principles, and the constitution laws of great nations!

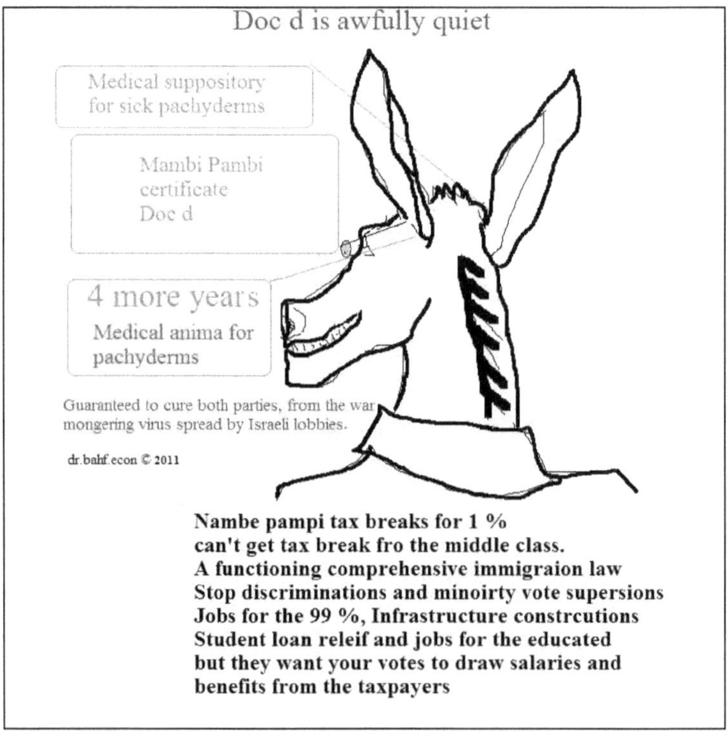

On this side of the murky pond, empty-headed political preachers have prematurely plagiarized completely the Euro-economic model of austerity, without a scintilla of research or evidence to back these imbecilities, out of felonious' habituation, or by mistake, if they admit to it, or worst by the anti-middleclass class-warfare design.[50] They have sprouted wishes, and hopes, and lies, and dishonest visions on these neo-Nazis, neocon, skinhead anti-immigration pro war visions, since the good old days. In misapplication of backwater legalism to immigration laws, with the self-deportation concept like self-genocide excuses of the Nazi camps, harassment of intellectuals, investors, CEOs of their job creators and other nationals, legal immigrants, they have imploded their local economies for years to come. Yet, in other little stupid actions, they have fallen backward on their own swords, hard enough that they cannot yet scream. Unfortunately, the quantity of mistrust, and twisted legalism injected in the laws and policies is so strong, that it will take major effort to retain entrepreneurs and highly skilled human capital to risk back the slings and arrows of such an economy, beside those type of regional anomalies.

They are men and genteel women, except for that little-known fact of slavery, and civil war and civil right movement, and years of vicious and immoral, anti-family, anti-Indians, anti-women, anti-minority, and anti-immigration policies they secretly covet by themselves in office, or by their hate-groups and dominium in backward states. American people cannot let them get away with these self-destructions. They have sunk the national dignities as low as it goes with their own popularity numbers. As matter of fact, the Europeans, Latinos or Asians, nor Muslims or Jews or Christians or theists, nor Agnostics or Atheists cannot let them destroy civilizations. It is no longer a matter of conservatism.

Their dark visions for an economic model, which only 10-20 percent of population had legal rights, and others were enslaved to feed the king rats, is an imbecilic nightmare of ill minds long dead. They are as anti-science and scientists, as they are anti-liberty and freedom, their resurrection in economic down turns, only identifies their felonious sources and their ill origins.

All descent people have to confront their illogical infamy as we confront Al-Qaeda, or other anti-modern-genocidal lawless terrorists, Klan, Tribes, or Cult, and militarists' psychos domestically and globally. They all remain the prominent American BenLadenists and have to be intellectually confronted that way. They are not honorable soldiers, they do not use honor codes of decent soldiers, or USA military code of conduct, Geneva conventions, or humane code of ethics, Theology is not set of ethical doctrine to them, it is a white hood. They use it to hide intent. They are not true conservatives. They are radical interventionists for cash. They have shown us that repeatedly for the last ten to thirty years or more. Their innate hate of constitutional laws has been more than intent. It has been demonstrated, documented shown in front of our own eyes.[51] Their disrespect for civility and traditional institutions has been repeatedly demonstrated.

They are right, you either on the side of constitutional law and ethical behaviors or on their side? If you are not on their side, you have to assign independent councils and keep away from further self-contaminations from a long list of constitutional law violations and war crimes. Their way has twisted two initial victories into global embracement and defeats, enlarged the numbers, ranks, and resolve, of theologically resolute enemies of Islam and humanity, it has given more than comfort to the wrong scallywags of history.

Yes, they have failed in big ways, and they want to hide that fact with all other inconvenient bothersome facts, that bubbles up now and in the future. Let the sun light in, let independent counsel, judges, and public study these bills of tenders for what they are worth in the light. We do not need to coddle evil of gradual Stalinism in modern democracies out of fear, vengeance, or profiteering motivations. Let the Alt-right-wing nuts' roaches run and scream from the sun light of public scrutiny. However, they have to be called out, when we find substantial evidence of their crimes. Do not demure of dealing and discussing their mistreatments of immigrants, or imprisoning political prisoners, and minorities for commercial motivations.

Their way, war-profiteering apparatus will regenerate more of the old anti JFK-strategies, either entanglements without cause and results and inevitable defeat, or right out defamations and assassination mongering to cover for their final acts of insanities. They have tried the second strategy first and failed. Now they are trying the first. The intellectually alert Americans and civilized world cannot let them get away with this.

They took Lincoln, and JFK (Bobby and King) we will not give you another one. At no times, it is a bright idea to start from illegal (unconstitutional) premises, and proceed to bad laws to cover criminal misconducts. Then try to sell these as a good or legal notions or patriotic laws. That was and is foolhardy. That is what they are accusing legal immigrant trapped by their legalisms, multiyear delays, and self-deportation, southern strategy immigration policy! The torture gang, which had the full support of Utah-representatives, conspired in breaking the law. They are convicted in the court of public opinions, without even seeing a judge. They will serve a life sentence as Nixon did. Those who have initiated a series of unconstitutional state-laws from the premise of anti-civil laws, anti-constitutional laws, and of racial and national profiling will meet even a harsher penalty than public condemnations, no matter how they fool themselves and their cadres and dominions into lawlessness.

The notions of something bad, evil, catastrophic happened, therefore, we can break all these laws, conventions, legal practices, and ethical and moral premise is foolish in law and it is worst in the court of domestic or global public opinions. It is imbecilic in practice, and it will offend all senses and will backfire with disastrous results in blowbacks. Explain that logic to the police officers, now convicted for shooting civilians on the bridge in post Hurricane Louisiana. Those promised and fleeting glimpses of security, dignity, and hope will become falling stars faster than you can say Abu Gharib, GETMO, or sleeping Afghani children. It is important to keep great principles of decency developed in American laws in mind at all times. They are not toys and trinkets, in order to fool others. They are still governing principles, no matter how many southern strategies have sworn discombobulate the constitutional principles.

You either find your way to moderation and centralism and truer conservatism or fade in your honey well of history. American people will do with you what they should have down to Nixonism as the source of these <Neocons> dishonesties, corruptions, self-destructive, Leninist, Stalinists' jingoism, and massive deceptive misconducts, lies and economic implosions.[52] You can come out on special days to defend yourselves against the longer lists of war crimes and abuses of USA constitutional laws, election laws, and other misconducts.

Their way we all act, as Israeli defense agency operatives, propagandists, and advocates regardless of American national interests, or global sanity, and national and international security. The NEOCONS did it, and they are still denying it. Instead of independent, unbiased monitoring of peace, we have violated USA laws against export of anti-personnel bombs, phosphate bombs used on UN. We suppose to stumble from one genocidal insane war into another without questions, and enraged friends and foes alike.[53] We are supposed to condone threats and ultimatum with deadlines to attack and spread radiation on other civilian population.[54] One of the quickest way, to encourage Middle East countries to speed up their nuclear energy industries is to attacked them, or kill their scientists. Killing scientists is a new low in human war history. We are supposed to use UN sanctions for fig leaf or be called cowards and anti-Semites by known war criminals, peace killers (as they killed Izak Rabin) and baby killers and their paid spies in our nations and militaries, after we have violated UN laws for the wrong wars. After, they have violated every UN resolutions. Specially, those UN resolutions established against their nuclear war machinery of over 300 Israeli nuclear warheads, and further spread of desperation among civilian populations. These agendas will finally morph into a total religious war, far away from any principles.[55] No true American or any principled human being will comprehend it as national security interests.

Their way we will only morally and ethically further justify and add to enraged crowds to react more insanely in return! Historically, when the international laws of reciprocity have not been reciprocated in full? Why should we add to the insanity rather than subtract from it? Why should American taxpayer Jewish, Muslims, and gentiles always pay for land grabs, thieving, dispossessing, and spread of poverty, and victimizing of innocent civilians for any sides, colors, creeds, states? Why not transfer American funds to domestic job-development project in our big cities, until the two state solutions is back in full effect again, and these duplicitous sedations, and threats, and land grabs stop. No matter how many kisser politicians, Bible thumpers, and political cheap dates you have paid off by American taxpayers' money. You have tromped, hornswoggled, and ramrodded the last half dozen USA presidents. The American taxpayers are wising up to your ways, so behave!

Their way is not to have individually paid portable health insurance plans regardless of national and individual costs and multitude of bankruptcies. It is not to have portable health coverage by law. It is not to have true competitions in the health-free market, with at least one government-regulated player in the mix, against the regulatory and regional monopolist. Nevertheless, it is keeping a corrupted broken old bribe-machine for the bad old politicians. Just in case, the military-political-industrial-money complex machine peters out. They need to be jeered out of politics as Daniel Rostenkowski was, when elderly citizen had to pelt his car with eggs and tomatoes in Chicago to get his attention. We need a new health plan that works for the patients now, after the billions we have spent and all the bankruptcies around us.[56] We need it now. We do not need to dismantle it.

Their way is not to have a rational executive pay plan with caps and band of limitations-formulas. The executive pay-packages need limitations and caps. The pay packages are functionally related to operation sales, revenues, and productivity-wages as future demands. They are not in some infinite symbolic back yard game, or in a pissing contest of their own delusional values in phantom crony capitalism. The executive pay-packages should not deplete the shareholders and capital coffer of individual operations and consumers. The executive pay-packages cannot bankrupt too big to fail institutions, and unleash systemic risk on the whole economies globally, the new CEO-socialism. The executive pay-packages cannot introduce systemic risk into insurance, banking, auto, and real estate industries, and skin the taxpayers for their failures, and the billion dollars flash-cash vanishings.

Their ways go after rational legal immigration policies, which will bankrupt more of, agriculture, technology, entertainment, leisure and hotel and hospitality-service industries. Never mind, the fact that it will starve social security fund even more.[57] They have wanted to dismantle it all of these years. They will not change their predatory spots now.

Their way will further compound shortfalls of Medicare's fund. Their way, middle class pays their taxes, poor with soldiers, students with their student-loans, emigrants (legal and otherwise) pay fees, pay sales taxes, pay day-rates, and loan usury rates up to 300 percent of their principles. Their way, the student loans will cripple most productive and bright lights of any functioning economy, and after graduation, they go in the unemployment lines or debt-prisons (Arizona neo-peonage systems), if the wrong people are elected. Moreover, the one percent richest will not pay social security taxes or payroll taxes. Their taxes have dropped from 85 to 25 percent, but they want to pay only 15 percent. Therefore, the economy contracted, because the 75 percent real income-job solution did not grow at the natural rate, or 3.5 percent rate. Their supply-side tinkle-down economy run out of tinkles decades ago.

Your health care plan that benefits you the most, your portable single payer plan is socialism shall not be mentioned ever. Their health care plans are tax deducted for income over $250,000, but yours will bring heck and damnation on USA. Never mind the senators' and congresspersons free health care plan, their Medicare plan are just fine, thank you. Theirs is not socialized medicine yours has to be. Get a clue! You, getting a decent job with livable wages will be socialism, they over charging, and multiple dipping in taxpayer pockets having free health insurance on your taxes is God sent, and it shall not be mentioned! Their 15 percent tax rate on privileged inside-information is self-sanctioned legal capitalism.[58] Yours is Godless communism, or European, and illegal insider trading.[59] Does any of this information sinks in, brothers and sisters, or am I preaching to the Phantom of the Opera, again? Takbir, Amen! Mind you, the 15 percent capital-formation tax-break was designed for the middle class step up, so we could grantee the American dream (the Utopic American Exceptionalsim), but like the other dream act, it became another legal tool in the lobbyists' toolbox for pretentious religiosity and patriotic jingoism, and a tax heaven for billionaires, the lobbyists' dystopia again.

Their way of breaking constitutional laws is not socialism, your pursuit of happiness, seeking god endowed constitutional rights is Socialism! What are these, the 50 million plus Americans, the working poor, the bankrupt middle class, students, and graduates that have no health insurance, no jobs? Who are the 14 to 25 million unemployed and under-employed? What are the 400,000 to 800,000 imprisoned immigrants, which are added to annually as laws are manipulated unconstitutionally to entangle and entrap legal immigrants and make them illegal, by legal and institutional predesigned deceits? Are they just socialists' champions? Are they the victims of illegal immigrants, but not the victims of your systemic thieveries for decades without accountabilities? Are they just collateral damages like in the villages of Afghanistan, or Iraqis' cities? No one needs to mimic your failed insane policies ever, unless they want to join you in the honey well of history. It is no civilized mezzanine. It is not the lighted castle on the hilltop, but Dante's art vision about the levels of hell.

Their take out of taxpayer to pay bankrupted big banks is biblically sanction theft and it is blessed, your old age pension, benefits is Socialism! You tell me, why did you vote them in? You have voted them in again, and again. On this Day take a minute and think for yourselves.

Many good people died for your freedom to think for yourselves and a few principles: constitutional laws, and bill of rights of all inhabitance on this dirt, starting with American Indians, to modern day populations. They were honorable soldiers on this Flag Day. Are you honest or honorable about anything? What have we given up to foreign and domestic terrorists, war profiteers, and fear mongers, and unfortunately to some medal mules? They are not conservatives. They do not believe in constitutional law, bill of right, or law. They do not honor bill of rights, or military honor codes of conduct. They are not ethical, or honest, they mislead the representative of this nation. They just do not believe in democracies. Does it matter if they put anything on their heads or they are a shade lighter, or they are medal mules? They are not really conservatives. Their deeds or misdeeds speak better than any labels. We cannot allow their evil ways of southern strategists to rise again! Moreover, it we will not. If they do not shape up and become friends of the people, servants of the public good as they promised, let us be done with them. Put in the term limits, from dogcatchers on to the senators.

They spied on us. They bankrupt us. They took away our constitutional rights. They have revoked our bill of rights. They sold their patriotisms and our constitutional protections to highest bidders, and cooperates' enterprises. The American people will banish you to the political oblivions until you prostrate your sorry dishonest plagiarists' souls on the gates of constitutional laws, bill of right, and individual rights and dignities.

Cat Callers' Uninformed Jeers

Catcalling Keynes and Economists, King Rats Are Talking! One hears political catcalls about J.M. Keynes! The economic teachings of E. Domar, I. Fisher, and J.B. Clark's are more apt economic-tools. They are more relevant for now. Especially, about the causes of wealth concentration and its follies, just in case, we ignored the historical economic-lessons of 1909, 1919, 1920s, downturns, we are reliving them.

The analysis of the diversions of IRS supplied adjusted gross income indices, for the top five e and ten percent top income earners, and the bottom 50 percent income earners (Figure 1), explains the sustained and planned effort behind wealth concentrations, which has been in effect since 1980s. The reconstructive economic remedies will be prolonged and very complex. Of course, such complexity need not confuse the imbecilic ideologues.

It is saving the rest of decent Americans that is still a concern to academics, while they are being squeezed financially, and being hounded by paid media manipulators, and their now obsolete voices.

There are no soft steps! What pained Ayn Rand is still with us today. Mega-Monopolists' "cooporatocracy" function parallel with Stalinism, familial dictatorships, and tin-cap totalitarianisms. They have methodically engaged in quiet and prolonged economic class warfare against middleclass, in order to transfer their tax load to fees and taxes, and legal burdens to the middle class. They dilute all market signals. They subvert judiciary up and down the steps. They victimize the victims often minorities and immigrants, and blame them for their self-destructive binges and extreme upward wealth misdistributions. They pervert representative democracies, and the military-political-industrial complexes for war profit gains, instead of expansive, diverse, and inclusive domestic job-creation strategies and sustainable economics.

Infrastructures

They have underfunded infrastructures rebuilding stimulus. They cheat any governing authority of its tax shares and revenues, by shifting tax earned benefits up, and tax burdens down. Tax breaks at the expenses of infrastructures, defense, the middle and lower classes earned benefits and healthcare are here. The burdens, costs, taxes on the working poor, and the middle managers, teachers, police, firefighters, to anybody and everybody have increase.

These empty vessels are accusing some dead-white person, with a British accent that has been dead for 6 decades! Other than ignorance, they are hate mongering against the Europeans' immigrant minorities, and they perverting the course of the republic, and representative democracy at home. Their imbecilic delusions are to milk the bull of cooporatocracy! American middle class, small businesses, and job-creationists will save the grace of American lives, if possible. Yes, some of the CEOs and cooperation will be there helping. Since, the reviving of aggregate demand will benefit them economically, too.

Here are two pictures depicting bad infrastructures examples.[60] This is to demonstrate and educate us, what comical infrastructures the opposition party has in mind for the future of our roads, bridges, and education in this country.

The austerity and sequestrations budgetary designs are more to damage the legacy of a sitting president, and protect the top wealth concentrators than to fix the economy confidence of investor class, or middle class. Systemic and chronic under-investment in education, infrastructures, and social-capitals is anti-investment, antigrowth.

Sustainability, in fiscal policy arena depends on the rebalancing of the equitable-taxation burden. Thereafter, equitable realignments can gradually reduce the debt. The debt mantra and austerity fundamentalists are on a vendetta against American level of living. They also have a sordid political agenda, under the supply side magic umbrella and over 30 years of their tinkle-down economic model.

Globally, under constrained economics, the sharp knives in the political air will fall on many victims. Those victims are the global middle class, where USA, Chinese, EU, and global aggregate-demand <~~is~~> was. Polemical and verbose leaders, at least in the relative democracies, will not last long, if they do not know how to use Job-creation in a sentence form. The usual calling-wolfs, terrorist suspects, 9-11 sloganeering, confusing Ben-Laden-ism with Islam, and reverting to Muslim hate instead of constructive criticism and dialogs about some of the bad Islamists' follies yield rotten fruits. Commonplace Joe-McCarty-ism (lefties, liberal, socialists, and communists), immigrant enslavements and neo-peonage laws, and misogynistic political women and minority bashings are not yielding the usual low hanging fruits, for the village idiots and rightwing political nuts. Even the slowest of their followers have figured it out after 30 years. John M. Keynes did not subvert the huge government cash infusion into TARP and quickly into their big investor bankers' pockets. Keynesians did not transfer stimulus money from the so-called nonexistent shovel-ready infrastructure jobs into cooperate coffers, and CEO bonuses, and multimillion dollar salaries instead of sustained multiyear multitudes of investments and jobs.

Keynes has been dead for six decades, he cannot even vote in Chicago again, for heck sakes, get over it. Their usual promised-Valhalla did not materialize so readily, because the middle class real disposable income is not there, because the same idiots took it and gave it to their bodies, and their political protection. Beside they have been mugging on any cheap camera and fixed news operators they can get to declare they are fighting against their elected president.

The lynching mobs have realized they had to pay for international shenanigans in one way or another, eventually. Moreover, here and now is the eventuality they sought. The technologies they covet, will undo "indo" your constitutional rights, and take away your jobs, not create new jobs. They have not created jobs yet. The high-flyers without paying taxes and after the 6-month obsolescence-cycles, they will be out of business, and their workers without unions or benefits will be out of work, and on middle class taxpayers good graces, while CEOs are declared billionaires, and global entrepreneurial leaders. They have had 30 years of it! The taxes they do not pay will come right out of your FICA, your paychecks, your take home pay. Your diminishing real disposable income decay for the last 30 years is your proof, every Friday, or out of the end of the month paychecks. Since, Presidents' Kennedy, Reagan, and two Bushes, the tax-rates have come down from 95 percent to about 25 percent, the cooperation strategies their way to pay 15 percent, still there are a good number of these mega-cooperation with billion-dollars of profit, which manage to pay no taxes. They have plenty of cash to pay lobbyists to reduce their taxes, so how low can they go. Well, that is when the subsidies kicked in. Thus, Central park New York addresses receiving substantial agricultural subsidies, the oil companies receive billions in subsidies, which are called a negative effective tax rate. However, academic tenures, decent salaries, educational, research, and development funding will bankrupt the government.

You can imagine a few oil-companies that have managed to pay close to zero tax rates, and received billion-dollars in subsidies, and then they cause a disaster, which wipes out a third of the national food industry and its related tax revenues. Moreover, they forced unemployment of a major region of American economy. Imaging a few nuclear energy industries doing the same thing in another country, which took out about a third of that country and oceanic resources, made them toxic waste for the unforeseeable future, unemployed that economic zones for long time. Nevertheless, who really pays the true costs of these disasters? Imagine in the meantime, their long war policies, has tripled the health cost of veterans from 23 billion to over 54 billion-dollars, (2010-2011 $ figures). Guess whose budget will take cuts in any budget deals, and whose burdens add to social security and Medicare burdens, instead of any tax adjustments on the upper 10 percent income earners, and a cooperate minimum tax rate for the companies making over 10 million. Do you still think they should not pay a cooperate-minimum-tax rate to aid with the affairs of democracy, defense, veterans, public education, unemployment benefits, job-creations, and domestic infrastructure?

Job Creation Can Help

Let study an economic problem, you can solve it with simple math. You can use your fingers and toes. Divide 14 trillion dollars ($14, 000 000 000 000.00 the mostly republican deficits) into 302 million people, that is $46, 360.00 per capita debt in USA. Take (25 million that are the unemployed), assumed they are employed at $50,000 times 15 percent tax rate minus standard deduction, 4500 x 25 mil. It is equal to $112,050,000,000 time that with 10 years and then 30 years. For the 30 years, you will have $3,361,500,000,000.00 that is over three trillion dollars revenue inflow for the government.

Well you are on your way to solve the USA deficit problem. Now add a 6 percent minimum tax rate to cooperate incomes, for over 10 million dollars cooperation, well almost a surplus appears In less than 30 years, which it took to wreck the economy, last time it was fixed. Finish one of those trillion dollar-wars, wow, get ready to be canonize, the Vatican is calling, or is it the Nobel Prize Committee, it could be the publishing clearinghouse. Yes, no republican will give $50,000 job to the chronically unemployed, the GOP wants him, or her self-deported, on mass, no question asked. They even do not want to pay long time teacher, professors, workers their retirement, they call it legacy hangovers. They are just happy plagiarizing what they can get they hand on, misinterpret the information, and blame everyone else when it will not work for them. Now, you are becoming too educated, you can understand the down side of Keynesians' paradox of miserliness. That is, why Hooversim is not a good economic growth model out of any economic recession, or depression. See you are already too educated for your own good. President Hoover was a nice man of commerce, and you could have stayed uneducated, and happy.

In this election more so than any other for some time, American voters will face a clausal decision to save their jobs, lives, their children, and their communities. The crooked mortgagors, the international institutional derivatives-paddlers, and student loan usuries were not the victims' faults. The victims did not bribe the congressional representatives and the senators to refit the laws, heck, even trash some laws, and make their own laws. The student did not lobby to raise the 3 percent student loan interest rates and accommodating rules, to 8 and 9 percent rates and payday contract laws. They did not pay lobbyists to modify Glass-Steagle act and many other laws. They did not pervert and twist the institutions' laws and mega-banks' mortgage rules. They did not fight or pay billions to lobbyists to fight the derivatives' regulations and enforcements of financial laws! They had no intentions of respecting or following the Laws. Those were done, top-down, trickle down, and tinkle down by supply-siders for trillions of dollars. Moreover, they are not paying taxes to expand the safety nets, essential for their victims. Those bad old days of elitists' political groups of 700 or 800 moneymen wrecking the country, prolonging unnecessary wars, breaking the laws, and hiding behind secret walls have been digitally removed. What remains is the decency, grace, and will of the people, the decent Americanism, to confront the political dishonesties of the American BenLadenists' misrepresentations. The overt hate propaganda, in place of job creation, accountability, transparency, and a decent level of cooperate, and cooperate-lobbyists' and their political employees' appropriate citizenship, by way of a minimum cooperate tax rate for mega-cooperation who decided not to create jobs.

Keep on yanking on those one-armed bandits for the CEO bonuses' payoffs. The cheaters were and are top down in trillion-dollars. Americans need to worry about the elderlies' Social Security and Medicare, their school ages' schools and teachers, workers, their gardeners, and nurses, their hospitality staffs, hotel and motel house-cleaners. Their Hollywood stars and visiting guests, their firefighters, and their police officers, and professors, their incarcerated youth, their vanishing educated scholars, and the jobs they can create, they are all on the menu, with the rest of middle class America.

In *Teconomics,* the microeconomic and production theory of technological injection in economics is further developed. It is on technological and human development, 335 pages, © 2010. In the book Teconomics, (*Scientific Synthesis of Economics and Technology in Teconomics,*) Bahman Fakhraie PhD details multitudes of logical foundations for pre-ancient importance of Persia in the technological development of humanity.[61] The hypothesis does not depend on the One-Item fluid story in most modern works. The important of Persian, Chinese, and the

Middle East in modern thought-knowledge development is examined in this scholarly work. The book is a great read, and the study is very important. It is reflected in the following comparative of divisions of comprehension in modern times. There is an old line, restating the old line of Europhilic, and Greco-Romanic oriental romanticism, about the source of democracy. The source supposedly is the one war among numerous wars between, Athens' ancient forces and Persian Empire. It is an important introductory read. Nevertheless, the counter arguments have been presented ably.[62]

> The first nation to recognize my country was Morocco. In signing the Treaty of Tripoli in 1796, our second President, John Adams, wrote, "The United States has in itself no character of enmity against the laws, religion or tranquility of Muslims." And since our founding, American Muslims have enriched the United States. They have fought in our wars, they have served in our government, they have stood for civil rights, they have started businesses, they have taught at our universities, they've excelled in our sports arenas, they've won Nobel Prizes, built our tallest building, and lit the Olympic Torch. And when the first Muslim American was recently elected to Congress, he took

> the oath to defend our Constitution using the same Holy Koran that one of our Founding Fathers -- Thomas Jefferson -- kept in his personal library.
>
> So I have known Islam on three continents before coming to the region where it was first revealed. That experience guides my conviction that partnership between America and Islam must be based on what Islam is, not what it isn't. And I consider it part of my responsibility as President of the United States to fight against negative stereotypes of Islam wherever they appear.

Therefore, there are a lot missing in the trite none-academic, "One-item, silver-bullet" hypothesis, beyond the details of that old line.

Decentralization of thought and action under necessary, sufficient, sustainability conditions for governance and running multiple cultural centers and nations were an invention of the same Empire of Persia. Persian and Chinese written international trade treaties are indeed the first detail international trade contract in the known history. The Persian, Greco-Athenian, along with Chinese political economic fusions for centuries had gifted cultural, political, and culinary innovations, evolutions, and technologies to Western and global democracies out of cultural diffusions of the region during the initial known millenniums of human history.[63]

> As a student of history, I also know civilization's debt to Islam. It was Islam -- at places like Al-Azhar -- that carried the light of learning through so many centuries, paving the way for Europe's Renaissance and Enlightenment. It was Innovation in Muslim communities -- (applause) -- it was innovation in Muslim communities that developed the order of algebra, our magnetic compass and tools of navigation; our mastery of pens and printing; our understanding of how disease spreads and how it can be healed. Islamic culture has given us majestic arches and soaring spires; timeless poetry and cherished music; elegant calligraphy and places of peaceful contemplation. And throughout history, Islam has demonstrated through words and deeds the possibilities of religious tolerance and racial equality.

The historical benefits have not been west east one-way roads some of the younger intellects assume.

Saadi, a Persian poet wrote, never argue with propagandists, (spin-meistres, etc.), because if you even win the argument, you won it in the intellectual mud wrestling! Nevertheless, getting muddy is democracy. The timing is particularly bothersome, when three unfunded, misrepresented, and self-destructive wars in Middle East have unhinged and unbalanced American economy, and Most Middle Eastern political structures. Militarism is a limited use statecraft tool, if it does not become fatally parasitic to the domestic and the global trade and commerce. In addition, to other new developments, which we remain clueless about, after 250 billion a year budget items on "Intel-Mushrooms," and hapless ways to undo the constitution and political blame games. Instead of infrastructure investments, and job creation, which were the mandates of the government?

The wartime psychosis, in the other hand, mushrooms. The uncontrolled parasitic self-promotion of it harms, as it kills its host's economies. That comforts and prolongs brutal totalitarian governments. The Vietnam War swallowed President Lyndon Johnsons' administration domestic job and social agenda completely, even when it had passed its end-time. Nixon terminated the war. A war depression at this time will cut off all funds, including the generals' fat pensions as legacy costs, and their promised jobs at the defense -industry-political inroad multiple-dipping promised land. The same economy has to pay for a huge increase in care, from $ 23 billion to over $ 53 billion for veteran spotty health care. They will also need job creation in the same depressed economy, under harsher scrutiny.

Notes

[1] The quoted phrase is credited to, an in memoriam of the late great conservative-speech writer of President Nixon Area, and a steam New York Time columnist, Mr. William Safire, which I met a few time.

[2] Paul Kennedy's 1988 book, The Rise and Fall of the Great Powers.
Michael Kinsley, ESSAY David Duke and American Decline, *Time,* Monday, Nov. 25, 1991, http://www.time.com/time/magazine/article/0,9171,974334,00.html

[3] The link is, http://shs.umsystem.edu/famousmissourians/leaders/dscott/dscott.shtml

[5] The freeman Institute, *Abraham Lincoln's Speech on the Dred Scott Decision,* http://www.freemaninstitute.com/lincoln.htm

[6] 18 USC § 1581 - PEONAGE; OBSTRUCTING ENFORCEMENT
(a) Whoever holds or returns any person to a condition of peonage, or arrests any person with the intent of placing him in or returning him to a condition of peonage, shall be fined under this title or imprisoned not more than 20 years, or both. If death results from the violation of this section, or

if the violation includes kidnapping or an attempt to kidnap, aggravated…

(b) Whoever obstructs, or attempts to obstruct, or in any way interferes with or prevents the enforcement of this section, shall be liable to the penalties prescribed in subsection (a)

More at: http://www.time.com/time/magazine/article/0,9171,954073,00.html#ixzz1mNSJGjMe

[7] Douglas A. Blackmon, *Slavery by Another Name: The Re-Enslavement of Black People in America from the Civil War to World War II*, Doubleday Publishing, March 25, 2008

[8] The individual in this video was murdered by USA uniform agents.

"On May 28, 2010, 24-year-old Ashley Young was on a pedestrian bridge along the San Diego-Mexico border when she heard a man below crying out for help. In a nearby U.S. Customs and Border Protection holding area, Young saw what she says was a man on the ground being beaten and tased by agents. She found the scene so troubling that she took out a camera..."

http://www.pbs.org/wnet/need-to-know/video/video-i-think-i-witnessed-someone-being-murdered/13687/

[9] "Because border agents <& ICE> are part of the Department of Homeland Security, they are not subjected to the same public scrutiny as police officers who use their weapons."

Brian Epstein, "Crossing the line at the border", *pbs.org*, April 20, 2012, http://www.pbs.org/wnet/need-to-know/security/video-first-look-crossing-the-line/13597/

[10] NINA BERNSTEIN, "Officials Hid Truth of Immigrant Deaths in Jail," *The New York Times*, http://www.nytimes.com/2010/01/10/us/10detain.html?_r=1&pagewanted=print

[11] Caveat Emptor, AZ papers-please Law
"MSNBC The Rachel Maddow Show - 26 April 2010, (& May, 2012) reported on the Arizona "immigration" law. Republican state senator Russell Pearce, who circulated a white separatist e-mail screed, and who also got caught on tape hugging a neo-Nazi, introduced it. The guy taking credit for writing the law is Kris Kobach, a birther running for secretary of state in Kansas, and who is an attorney for the legal arm of FAIR, an "immigration reform" group whose founder, John Tanton, argued in 1986 about whites being out-populated by non-whites." They are also proponent of self-deportation logic, in using legalism and power authority (<by brown-shirts?>) to intimidate people to give up their rights, with some Republican Mormon political activists supports, whom are running for high office. While other Mormons, have been fighting against their xenophobic and racists extremisms. The Law also added build in immunities for FAIR, against legal actions. Now, they are imposing on the Supreme Court to expand and legitimize their political intends, as a Republican Party legitimate movement. So that their Neo-Nazi, Neocons dream government can take shape, and they can purify American government, academia, and the courts! We saw that movie with subtitles before. Just say Nein, NO!
http://www.democraticunderground.com/discuss/duboard.ph

p?az=view_all&address=385x459609
http://www.democraticunderground.com/discuss/duboard.ph
p?az=view_all&address=385x459609

[12] "Mr. Weber wrote that he believed the agency had handled Mr. Bah's case appropriately. "However," he added, "I also don't want to stir up any media interest where none is warranted." Helping to bury Mr. Bah overseas, he wrote, "will go a long way to putting this matter to rest."
In the agency's confidential files was a jail video showing Mr. Bah face down in the medical unit, hands cuffed behind his back, just before medical personnel sent him to a disciplinary cell. The tape shows him crying out repeatedly in his native Fulani, "Help, they are killing me!", Ibid

[13] "...According to records The Times obtained in December, one Eloy detainee who died, in October 2008, was Emmanuel Owusu. An ailing 62-year-old barber who had arrived from Ghana on a student visa in 1972, he had been a legal permanent resident for 33 years, mostly in Chicago." Ibid

[14] Mercedes Exec Arrested Under Ala. Immigration Law Nation's strictest anti-immigrant measure gets fresh scrutiny amid xenophobia claims.
Will Oremus, *Exec Arrested Under Ala. Immigration Law*, Posted Monday, Nov. 21, 2011, at 7:48 PM ET
http://slatest.slate.com/posts/2011/11/21/mercedes_benz_executive_arrested_under_alabama_immigration_law.html
Huffingtonpost.com, *German Mercedes-Benz Executive Arrested Under Alabama's New Immigration Law*, Posted: 11/22/11 12:17 AM ET

http://www.huffingtonpost.com/2011/11/22/german-arrested-alabama-immigration-law_n_1106870.html

[15] Verna Gates, *Alabama immigration crackdown nabs Mercedes executive,* BIRMINGHAM, Ala | Tue Nov 22, 2011 1:14am EST http://www.reuters.com/article/2011/11/22/us-immigration-alabama-mercedes-idUSTRE7AL0DT20111122

[16] "(Reuters) - As Mercedes-Benz executive … negotiated the streets of Tuscaloosa last week, he drove right into the controversy over Alabama's tough new immigration law. The rental car he was driving, lacking a tag, caught the attention of a local policeman, who stopped Hager on Wednesday. When the officer asked for a driver's license, all he had on him was a German ID card.
"He was taken into custody," Tuscaloosa Police Chief Steven Anderson said.
Under Alabama's new immigration law, considered the toughest in the nation, everyone in Alabama must carry a valid identification card, including U.S. citizens. Before the new law, a citation would have been issued and the driver would have been sent on his way. Now offenders are taken to jail, Anderson said." Ibid

[17] There is the comprehensive immigration law. The streamlining and expediting of current cases and new cases, the expanded dream acts for all graduates, all higher degrees, and all professional investors, entrepreneurs, and expedited family unification will clear the backlogs. Most of these will reduce the costs and care of children citizens, if we get off the short term parsimonious reductionisms, and inhumane notions, assertions and xenophobic false claims, and rampant and rancid political demagoguery.

[18] Attorney Daryl Williams, presentation in his amicus briefs with the supreme court and the following links have more related arguments. http://www.americanprogress.org/issues/2010/04/arizona_facts.html

[19] Michael Kinsley, ESSAY David Duke and American Decline, *Time,* Monday, Nov. 25, 1991, http://www.time.com/time/magazine/article/0,9171,974334,00.html

[20] Mike Lillis, *Democrats join DOJ suit against Alabama immigration law*, 11/22/11, 02:56 PM **ET**

[21] Economist, *Immigration, Crying wolf, The Republicans are fretting about a disappearing problem*, Nov 19th 2011, http://www.economist.com/node/21538750/

[22] Josh Gerstein, *Justice Department sues over Arizona immigration law,* 7/6/10 2:18 PM EDT, Updated: 7/7/10 11:49 AM EDT, http://www.politico.com/news/stories/0710/39413.html

23

http://www.nytimes.com/2011/07/26/world/europe/26oslo.html?_r=1&hp

http://www.nytimes.com/2011/07/25/us/25debate.html?src=me&ref=general

[24] Economist, *Migration and business, Weaving the world together*

Mass migration in the internet age is changing the way that people do business
http://www.economist.com/node/21538700/

[25] it is rare voice, but it is there.

[26] This article was written on March 10, 2012, after a series of devastating tornado, and loose talk of preemptive wars, again. It was adopted to include in this book.

[27] Benjamin Netanyahu, PM speech to Israeli-USA lobbyist, 5 March 2012, http://www.algemeiner.com/2012/03/05/full-text-of-netanyahu-speech-to-aipac-2012/

[28] IKE and JFK informed Americans and the world about these bad designs.
http://www.youtube.com/watch?v=GR5m1-5ksj0&feature=related

[29] I am sure the citizen-decision of the Supreme Court did not see that coming, as we will not see problems with the strip-search-decision. All honorable men and women in the incarcerations-industries and police forces equally respect minors and minorities in the system. I hope the honorable jurors will visit and inspect the hospitality of the same systems.
I think the American people see from the bird eyes view better, when the seek term limits.
http://news.yahoo.com/strip-searches-supreme-courts-disturbing-decision-101205560.html
http://www.latimes.com/news/nation/nationnow/la-na-nn-oregon-man-strips-down-to-protest-tsa-20120418,0,7286588.story

[30] UK, high office-public servants (Prime Ministers, with some International Intrigues, therefore these are inclusive with other ministries? Scotland Yard and police, private detective agencies are used in coordinated criminality and overt violations against civil and private lives of citizens). Some investigations have taken place on three continents.
a-http://www.pbs.org/wgbh/pages/frontline/murdochs-scandal/
USA, anti-Muslim hate crimes, and multiple wars, are used to cover up the links between the corruptive influences of the same Medias bad actors, money, methods, and the rights' high office-fandangos, nationally and internationally, appear very similar. No complete investigations of the money-links have taken place yet. FBI is supposed to be on this job, too! The public anticipation has been building up for the discoveries and disclosures, after we hear it all from the Wikileaks, again!
b-http://www.pbs.org/wgbh/pages/frontline/foreign-affairs-defense/are-we-safer/docs-reveal-fbi-used-muslim-outreach-as-guise-to-collect-intel/
c-http://www.pbs.org/wgbh/pages/frontline/religion/man-behind-mosque/america-and-muslims-by-the-numbers/
Israeli-Iran War
http://www.foxnews.com/story/0,2933,461588,00.html
Dishonest claims are abound, not as much psychological disinformation, but pathological misinformation are used to hide national and international criminalities.
"Azerbaijan denies granting Israel access to air bases on Iran border
A Foreign Policy magazine report on Wednesday claimed Israel was given access to Azerbaijani air bases in the event of an Iran strike."
By **Haaretz** published 18:32 29.03.12 Latest update 18:32 29.03.12

http://www.haaretz.com/news/diplomacy-defense/azerbaijan-denies-granting-israel-access-to-air-bases-on-iran-border-1.421562

[31] They forget that they are the proof of separations of church and state. However, past presidents state it more succinctly. This is JFK's pre-election speech on Church and State. All want-to-be presidents should know it by heart.
http://www.youtube.com/watch?v=iDP4qrA8hvg

[32] D. Nakamura and E. O'Keefe, "*Inquiry points to wider Secret Service scandal involving as many as 21 women,*" *USA TODAY*, 4, 17, 2012,
http://www.usatoday.com/news/washington/story/2012-04-17/secret-service-scandal/54349978/1

[33] D. Stanglin, "U. S. condemns troops posing with bodies of suicide bombers," *USA TODAY,* 4, 18, 2012,
http://content.usatoday.com/communities/ondeadline/post/2012/04/us-officials-condemn-photos-of-troops-posing-with-bodies-of-suicide-bombers/1

http://www.nytimes.com/2012/04/19/world/asia/us-condemns-photo-of-soldiers-posing-with-body-parts.html

[34] JFK's pre-election speech is on Church and State.
http://www.youtube.com/watch?v=iDP4qrA8hvg

[35] Zbigni's new book "Second Chances" is a good read on ZEITGEST, and recent three decades of international foreign policy issues.
http://www.nytimes.com/2007/03/06/books/06kaku.html?ref=zbigniewbrzezinski&pagewanted=print

[36] It is important to hear voices of reasons.

"New York Cardinal Timothy Dolan, saying that as a Catholic she felt the bishops should highlight the injustices she and others saw in the Republican plans.
"What I am asking for is a campaign for the poor, the hungry, the middle class, the people who are going to be eviscerated by the Ryan budget," DeLauro told Catholic News Service.
That same day, some 60 Catholic social justice leaders, theologians and clergy also released a statement saying that "this budget is morally indefensible and betrays Catholic principles of solidarity, just taxation and a commitment to the common good."
Tuesday's statement from the bishops came the same day as Bishop Stephen E. Blaire of Stockton, Calif., called a proposed cut in benefits for children of immigrants "unjust and wrong." Blaire, chairman of the bishops' Committee on Domestic Justice and Human Development, also decried any cuts in food stamps while preserving federal subsidies for industrial farming enterprises."
David Gibson, "Catholic Bishops Say Ryan Budget Fails Moral Test," *Huffington Post,* Religion News Service, Posted: 04/18/2012 1:32 pm Updated: 04/18/2012 1:32 pm http://www.huffingtonpost.com/2012/04/18/ryan-budget-catholic_n_1434919.html

[37] Former President Jimmy Carter's new book, "*Palestine: Peace Not Apartheid,*" is interviewed from his home in Plains, Georgia. He responds to a caller who asks questions concerning pressure put on the US political system and the resulting support of Israel. http://www.youtube.com/watch?NR=1&v=uvtC_qzHVM4&feature=endscreen

[38] Germany is grasping with its historical guilt and a newly imposed involvement in the global wars by rearming with nuclear subs, belligerent violators of international laws and treaties, and its political neophytes are attaching its <bad?>old salts. This article is about Günter Grass's poem. What is a democracy, which cannot tolerate freedom of speech?
Jakob Augstein, "Why We Need an Open Debate on Israel," *SPIEGEL online,*
http://www.spiegel.de/international/world/0,1518,druck-826180,00.html

[39] The exodus Christians of the *Holy Land* finally found proper viewing, promised by freedom of speech amendment. The paragons of only self-declared democracy in ME could not stand for it.
ttp://www.cbsnews.com/video/watch/?id=7406228n&tag=api&fb_ref=belowVideo&fb_source=home_multiline
"Last Sunday, 60 Minutes ran a segment entitled "Christians of the Holy Land,"with Bob Simon, shedding light on the struggles of Palestinian Christians living under Israel's occupation. In the segment, Palestinian Christians affirm their commonality with Palestinian Muslims in suffering under and struggling against the same oppression. The segment also includes an interview with Israeli Ambassador to the United States, Michael Oren, which exposes how the Israeli government tried to censor the story."
Rusty Pipes Follow, "Thank You, 60 Minutes!", *dailykos.com*, Thu Apr 26, 2012 at 03:17 PM PDT, http://www.dailykos.com/story/2012/04/26/1086323/-Thank-You-60-Minutes-

[40] Iranians remember the empty promises of advancement and development form Tehran treaty accord, signed from Stalin, Churchill, and FDR.

[41] President Eisenhower would not get involved in an attack on Egypt's Suez, after AJAX, in Iran, for British and Israeli interests. President Dwight Eisenhower's Farewell Address to the nation January 17, 1961, (IN FULL), http://www.youtube.com/watch?v=CWiIYW_fBfY

[42] Watch the link, it is funny, John Steward http://www.huffingtonpost.com/2011/03/05/utah-immigration-law-appr_n_831846.html

[43] On PBS, Need to Know", beating death of detainees http://www.pbs.org/wnet/need-to-know/security/video-first-look-crossing-the-line/13597/
On "MSNBC The Rachel Maddow Show - 26 April 2010, (& May, 2012) reported on the Arizona "immigration" law. Republican state senator Russell Pearce, who circulated a white separatist e-mail screed, and who also got caught on tape hugging a neo-Nazi, introduced it. The guy taking credit for writing the law is Kris Kobach, a birther running for secretary of state in Kansas, and who is an attorney for the legal arm of FAIR, an "immigration reform" group whose founder, John Tanton, argued in 1986 about whites being out-populated by non-whites."
They are also proponent of self-deportation logic, in using legalism and power authority to intimidate people to give up their rights, with some Republican Mormon political activists supports, whom are running for high office. While other Mormons, have been fighting against their xenophobic and racists extremisms. The Law also added build in immunities for FAIR, against legal actions.
http://www.democraticunderground.com/discuss/duboard.ph

p?az=view_all&address=385x459609
http://www.democraticunderground.com/discuss/duboard.ph
p?az=view_all&address=385x459609

44

http://www.nytimes.com/2010/01/10/us/10detain.html?pag
ewanted=all
http://fairimmigration.org/tag/immigrant-death-in-
detention/

45 "The documents, obtained over recent months by The Times and the American Civil Liberties Union under the Freedom of Information Act, concern most of the 107 deaths in detention counted by Immigration and Customs Enforcement since October 2003, after the agency was created within the Department of Homeland Security." NINA BERNSTEIN, "Officials Hid Truth of Immigrant Deaths in Jail," *The New York Times,* http://www.nytimes.com/2010/01/10/us/10detain.html?_r=1&pagewanted=print

46 Tobias Barrington Wolff, "The Republican War on Women: Invading the Vagina in Virginia," huffingtonpost.com Social Reading, Posted: 02/15/2012 10:31 am, http://www.huffingtonpost.com/tobias-barrington-wolff/virginia-ultrasound-bill_b_1278832.html

47 http://www.huffingtonpost.com/2011/03/05/utah-immigration-law-appr_n_831846.html

48 "Park City Police Chief Wade Carpenter will not cross-deputize his officers as immigration agents. And, on Friday, he labeled the new Utah law that outlines the practice as "window dressing" and a "knee-jerk reaction" to

a serious problem. "I don't think it accomplishes what we need to accomplish," Carpenter said Friday. "It's the tail wagging the dog." Summit County Sheriff Dave Edmunds also said his deputies will not participate in the program put forth in SB81, sponsored by Rep. Mike Noel, R-Kanab. Earlier this week, officials of Salt Lake City said its police department also would not cross-deputize officers as immigration agents."
Christopher Smart, *The Salt Lake Tribune*, Updated 04/10/2009 04:54:33 PM MDT, "More law enforcers declining to follow state immigration statute."

[49] Department of Justice Challenges Utah's Immigration Law
Several Provisions Interfere with Enforcement of Federal Immigration Law, Tuesday, November 22, 2011
http://www.justice.gov/opa/pr/2011/November/11-ag-1526.html
Monday, October 31, 2011
Department of Justice Challenges South Carolina's Immigration Law
Complaint Cites Conflict with Federal Enforcement of Immigration Laws
http://www.justice.gov/opa/pr/2011/October/11-ag-1429.html

[50] http://www.pbs.org/wgbh/pages/frontline/murdochs-scandal/

[51] http://www.youtube.com/watch?v=LP55l6DtgkY, http://www.youtube.com/watch?v=jgVl8LbBuPE

[52] http://www.youtube.com/watch?v=H1n00siTGHw

[53] http://rt.com/news/iran-israel-nuclear-threat-557/

[54] http://rt.com/news/israel-paradigm-iran-baruch-783/
http://rt.com/news/iran-israel-strike-panetta-425/

[55] That unfortunate total-war will lead to in-kind retaliations, which will not exclude uses of retaliatory nuclear devises. We all have been aiming, praying to delegitimize.

[56]http://www.scandalthecardgame.com/scandals.html#2002

[57]http://www.newsweek.com/2011/01/30/america-s-deporter-in-chief.print.html

[58] "A 2004 academic study based on trades by senators from 1993 to 1998 found that taken together, the senators' portfolios beat the market by a whopping 12 percent per year."
By James O'Toole, *Congress takes on insider trading ... by Congress,* CNNMONEY, December 7, 2011: 10:07 AM ET,
http://money.cnn.com/2011/12/07/news/congress_insider_trading/index.htm

[59] With political speed the stock bill BAN was passed, and signed by president on 4/4.2012.
"A 2006 bill, the Stop Trading On Congressional Knowledge (STOCK) Act, aimed to hold politicians to the same standards as corporate insiders. It got little support."
Economist, *Insider trading and Congress, Capitol crimes, Congress considers legislation to limit its own insider trading,* Dec 10 th 2011,
http://www.economist.com/node/21541434

There was a 60 minute CBS news show about this subject

[60] Comical representation of infrastructures was an open untitled source, minimally cropped from internet for educational demonstration.

[61] Intellectual source of religious tolerance and early writing are presented, with a diversion from factual details or early spins in ancient history of Persian artifacts. http://www.youtube.com/watch?v=QpmsftF2We4&feature=share

[62] President Barack Obama, Text of speech at Cairo University, the White house, June 4, 2009. The Associated Press The Associated Press Thu Jun 4, 3:58 pm ET, 2009

[63] Ibid

CHAPTER 3

Neocon Capitalism versus Free Competitions Capitalism

Neocon capitalism is not the same thing as free enterprise capitalism. Neocon capitalism had been practiced for the last three decades under the table to fool the victimized western economies, and the middle class and working classes. The unfunded forever wars, the deficit does not matter long wars were new chapters. The risk and trust destructions will not influence international trade, finance, and investments economy, too big to let fail banking and finance model, real disposable income of middle class does not matter, as long as the top one percent pretenders get everything.

Neocon Capitalism is a fraudulent notion. It is not a functioning economic model. It is not even a good economic proposition, let alone a hypothesis. It has been fighting tooth and nail the reparatory attempts of free enterprise democratic capitalisms. They confiscated supply-siders' buzz words as a camouflage, as they fronted defense and patriotic fervors to supplant the constitutional protection of citizens. The retrogressions will come later, when their subterfuges are not needed. Moreover, they have manipulated enough laws, in order to combat publics in the democracies. First victimizing the victims, underclasses minorities, announced and denounced enemies, and others, but later, they start monitoring and confiscatory policies about all people. It may be later now.

Gross Domestic Product Rate

It is important to study the real numbers, or the true changes in the real numbers, which reflect general notion of economic activities. The academic exercise is to show what kind of policy can remedy what ills, if there are any. In four decades since 1970, we have had six episodes of near zero or negative rate of growth of real GDP.[1] The last one 2008-2009 particularly was a nasty drop, since you have all felt it. Figure 5 shows rates an annual growth and decay rate of RGDP, 1970-2009. Figure 6 shows a more detail study of real and nominal GDP, for 1929 to 2016.

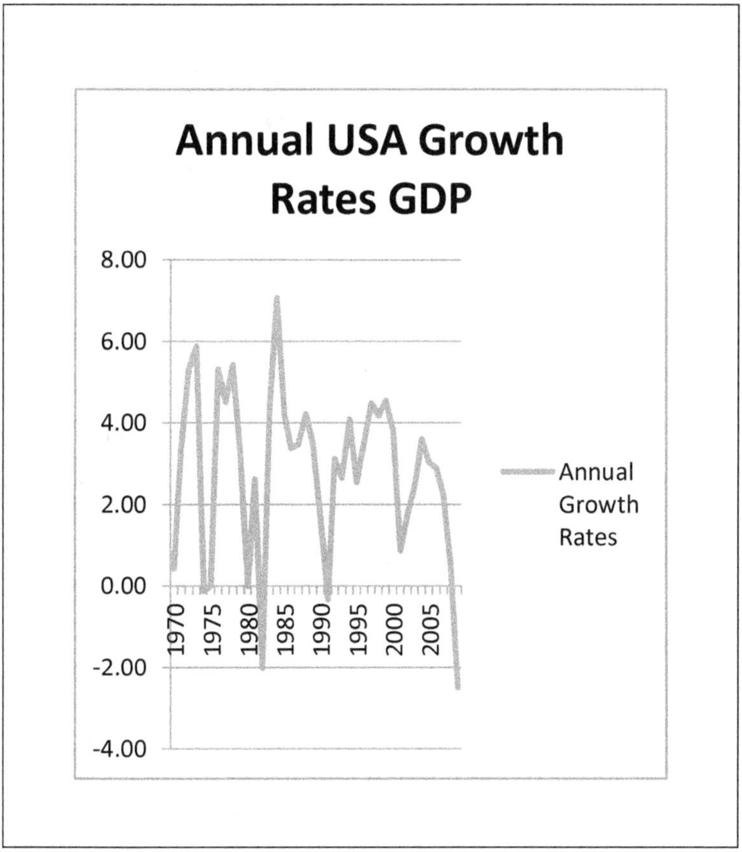

Figure 5, Annual growth and decay rate of RGDP, 1970-2009

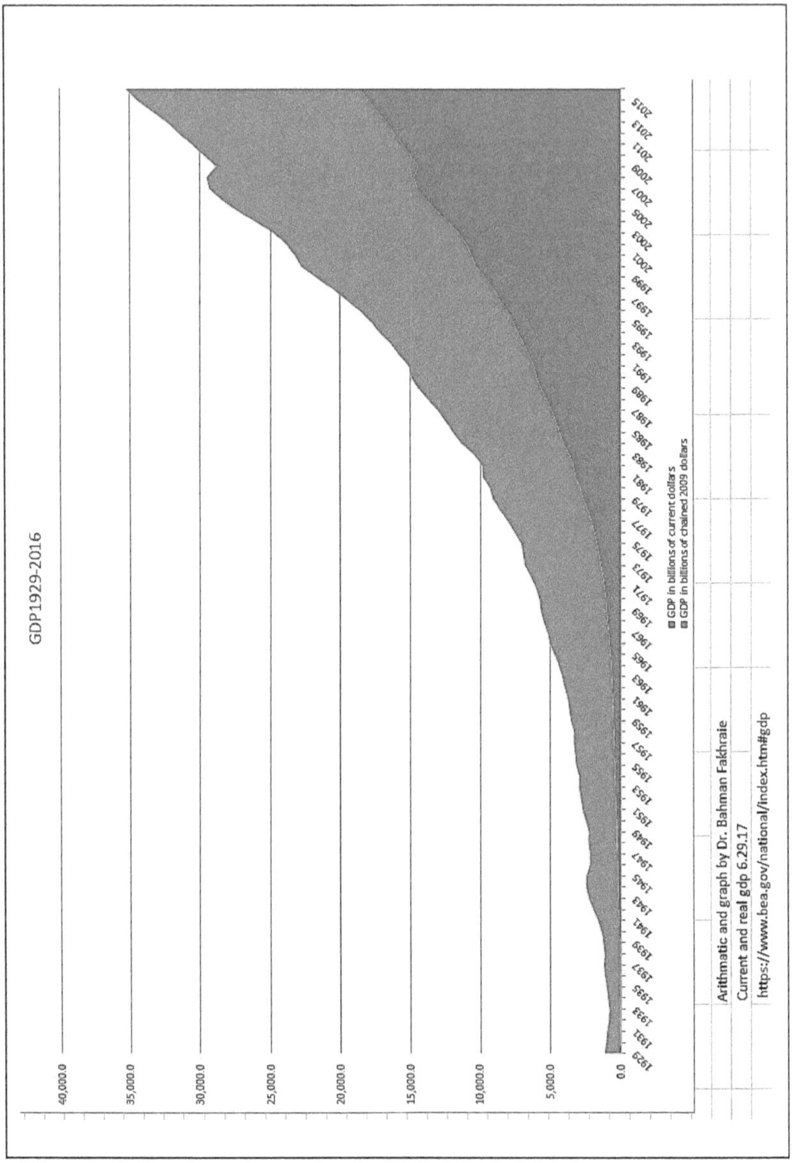

Figure 6, Real and nominal GDP 1929-2016

Figure 7 shows the real rate of growth and decay for the same data for 1929-2016.

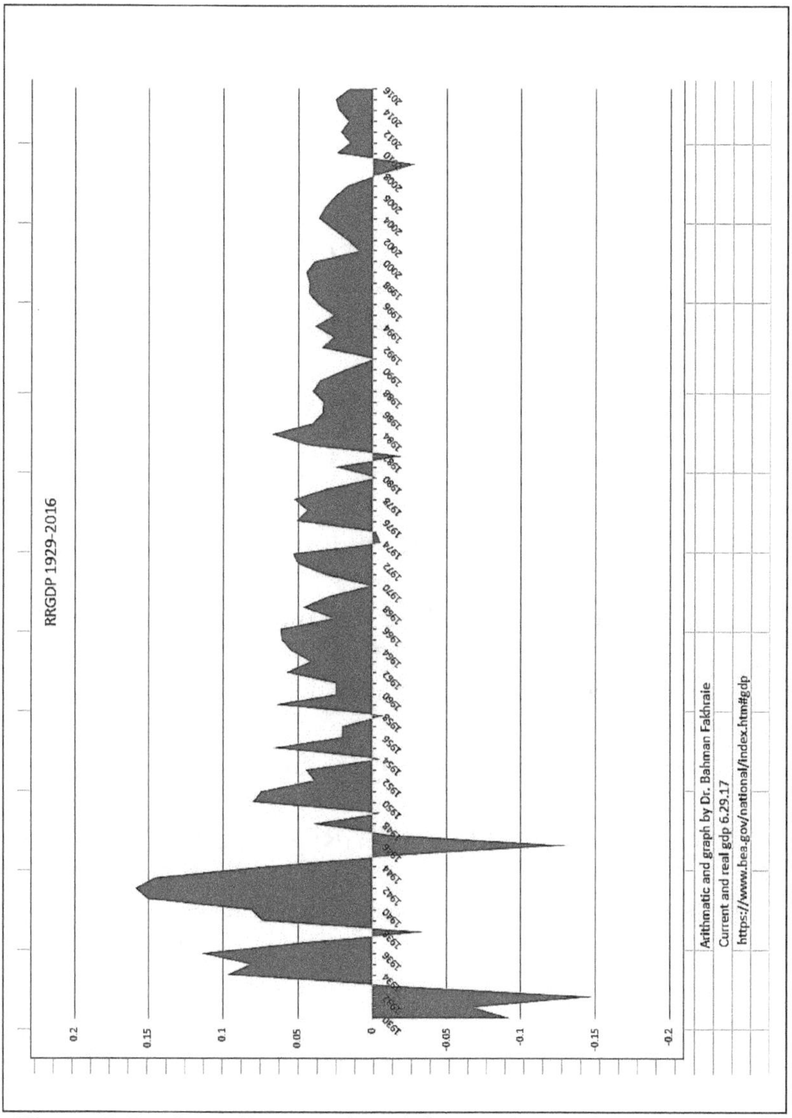

Figure 7, Real rate for growth and decay of GDP for 1929-2016

That is why burdening the consumers, or demand side of the economy will be extremely magnified, and very counterproductive. This combined with the few decades of upward mal-redistributions of income make a volatile mixture for stable economic growth even for marginal economic recoveries. So that fear of inflation can be used as an excuse, to stop halfway, and avoid the real recovery of the middle class, and even poor out of the economic recessions.

Nevertheless, the index illusions show that there were periods of growth. Therefore, the next cyclical shock will be harsher, harder, and lower. That is when normal remedies fall short. That is why the full double barrel job creation via infrastructure and TARP saving of big bad bank had to be coupled up and followed one after the other.

Neocon Capitalism

For	Against
Cooperate-welfare	Educators
Megbank bailouts	Living wage,
Unfunded long wars	Legacy Union pentions
Tax Breaks for the 1%	Middleclass fees and taxes

That is why dysfunctional houses of representatives could not or did not do. Neocon capitalists' financiers wanted to undo social security, Medicare, healthcare, but that is a disequilibrium force. They wanted forever wars for Israel and friends, for "freedom, liberty, and democracy" for mushroom clouds in our living rooms, in Africa, in Asia, but United State national security interests somehow vanished, or subsumed by these other paid PACs, and lobbyists' interests. In addition, they passed laws to suppress the minority votes, immigrant votes, women vote. They used the security fears to pass voting cards, with great new fees, (another poor and middle-class tax). Somehow, American voting became as driving license privileged law, not the divine law of American exceptionalism idea. That is another major disequilibrium, and a major destructive blow back, in the finances and economic conditions of the American taxpayers for doubtful, mercurial rewards, mainly tax break for the top earners. They wanted a minority president to take the blames of their subterfuges, so they called him Muslim and worst. That like buying the political offices does not always work either, unless the voters are really stupid, or scared out of their minds.

Growth Rate of Middle Class Taxes

They have taken middle class taxes and jacked up fees, and reduced productive workers ranks and numbers, for fake promises of job and increased real income, none of that has materialized, but the self-serving policies are constantly spanned as solutions. They are not. The following graph shows a more recent study of post-recession condition of individual income tax payers. Naturally, these would be reflected as clusters among the middle-class income tax payers, their aggregate gross income after taxes and the growth rate index of the same has dropped.[2] The data is from internal revenue service's historical data collection in current USA dollars, for 2004 to 2009. Figure 8 shows after taxed income.

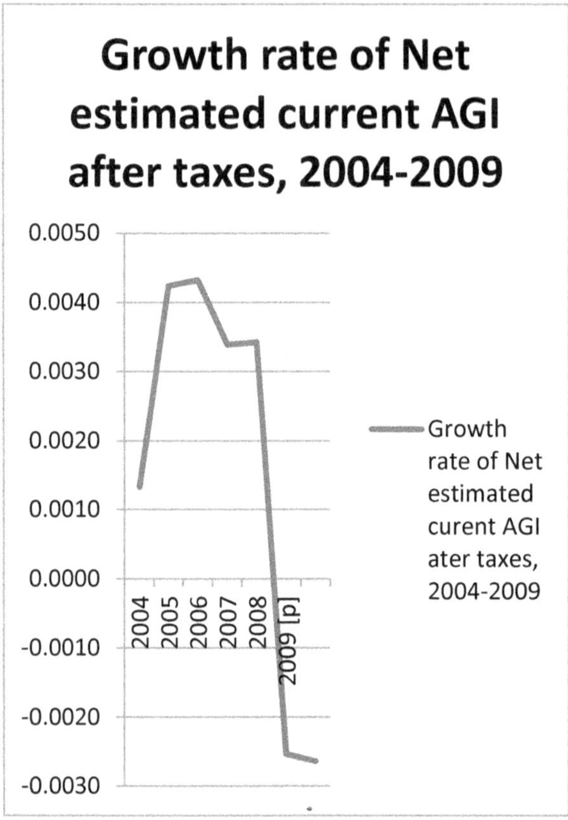

Figure 8, Growth and decay rates of after tax income for United States , 2004-2009

P indicates a preliminary number for 2009, and this graph is calculated in current dollars. The direction and severity of the decay rate are verified by other studies, and data and graphs, about growth and decay rates of GDP, and employment, and real or constant evaluation in this paper. For the budding economic scholars, which would like of duplicate or maintain such an index? For this kind of graph disposable real income values are calculated, except in this case, we are looking at the current condition, therefore, we are using the nominal values of disposable income. It is all income salary, wages, interest, rent, and government inflows, minus all out flows, less tax.

They take tax breaks supposedly for entrepreneurs, for capital formation, investors, and they have transferred it to money managers, hedge fund handlers' 15 percent flat tax. We have to be careful. Their notion of entrepreneurs will be robotics, a front crew, and hedge fund managers, and years of tax breaks on billions of dollars. That is the most dangerously preposterous, disequilibrium, unsustainable economic model of all human living history.

Even as a socialists' utopia it will implode and fail miserably into a dystopia.

The economy needs a balanced approach. Revenue increases and job creation to enhance the revenue increases, supply side expansions sustainably. If a few percent of population grab the good chunk of the revenue and go home to play with their marbles, and leave the economic activities to be sustained by fees and taxes from decreasing revenues of the middle class, declining, marginalized, and deported legal immigrants, the imbalances will spread. The economic activities will feel the shortfall in aggregate demand, and the real growth rate takes one of those six of seven dives, in the graph of real gross domestic products picturing the general economic activities. This is not a situation unique to Untied States, as you will read more about the global situation in this study.

The following book link, studies technological transfers to Western societies, for example transfers of book making, and linen paper technologies are detailed.[3] The research details that Persia-Chinese, Middle East, and Africa to Europe contributed extensively to the technological foundations and diffusions.[4] The essences of trade, commerce, diplomacy, and political exchanges evolved with human history. In half of dirty dozen states, the Americans may have to legally-fight to decertify some of their political parties, or sub-branches of their state's political parties, which persistently undo constitutional rights of other minorities and citizen alike, they victimize their workers, their teachers. I do not recall a book of polemic or even Eyan Rand's book, which encourages, or argues for a nihilistic version of conservatism, maybe the new model follows the one that their hero burns down the structure. This is the antithetical version of anything conservatism was purporting to present.

They connive and collude or go belligerent against their local newspapers to engage and encourage discriminatory practices, and group victimization, self-deportation of poor, very young, and very old legal immigrant Americans.[5] Those southern strategists would like to haul us back to pre-civil war days, with only 20 percent of the white male economy was legally able to operate, and functionally unable to meet demands, thus victimizing different classes of people as slaves. They had to shut out minorities and women by legal connivances, and unconstitutional criminalities, often with violence, legal terrorism, and physical attacks to maintain the unsustainable sociopolitical and economic model. They are surprised they are not trusted.

They only way to revive such an economically broken model is by giving loans and guarantees out to investors, entrepreneurs, and immigrant entrepreneurs to invest in such an economy. In other word, this will reduce the overt risks of confiscatory policies, haphazard deportations, which they have overtly adopted, and fanatically and misguidedly followed. Two examples of this model was tried, One was the first President Bush social-security-number tax credits nationwide, immediately after 9-11-2001, it worked. Two is the hand out by Treasury to major investment banks to cover mortgage swap-derivatives losses, the jury has jumped out of the window, but some of banks say" we did not need it, but thanks the taxpayers, middle class, but now pay more bank fees for our troubles of receiving it.

Here is a water well joke it may elucidate our plights. A seeker of wisdom climbed a mountain road to the see a Wiseman in the East. The seeker gets there in a windy day and sits patiently in front of the temple. The Wiseman hurries out and asks what he wants to know. Well Wiseman, I came to ask you about world peace and happiness. He got up and on his way back inside, and out of the wind, he said, "Never mind the Peace, and don't urinate into the wind, you'll stay happy." The seeker start walking down from the temple, he decided to test the wisdom of the received words. He started to urinate into the wind, and got it all over his cloth, so he turned around, and then he heard the Wiseman calling from the temple, “You imbecile, now you are doing it in our water well!”

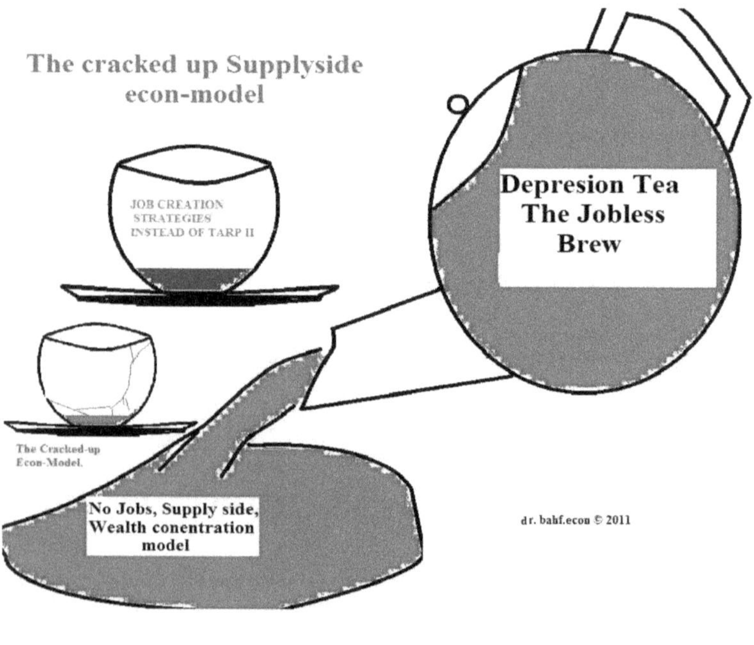

CHECK THE LABELS, BEFORE YOU DRINK IT!

In about these halves of dozen states, the Americans may have to legally-fight to decertify some of their political parties, or sub-branches of their state's political parties, which persistently undo constitutional rights of other minorities and citizen alike, they victimize their workers, their teachers.[6] Those southern strategists would like to haul us back to pre-civil war days, with only small percent of the economy being legally able to conduct business, and functionally unable to meet demands, thus victimizing different class of people as slaves, and shutting out minorities, legal immigrants, and women by legal connivances and unconstitutional criminalities.[7]

There has so rarely been such a time, which needed all Americans to call an end to these political mischiefs. Let their cooperate-bosses, their CEOs pay for them. We have had more than enough of their misdeeds. After thirty years of looking at the horses' rare-ends, and looking up the monkey tree, we must realize, that is where the stinks come from. It is not the economists employed or not, it is not Keynes 6 decade long dead. It is those, which have bamboozled us out of our affordable health care, less carbon-intensive transportation, and lifelong retirement benefits, and a decent salary to pay for them, but they keep theirs. We need to terminate their services along with fast track term limits for all political offices. The nature of transactional political capital being what it, long terms hopes of sustainable solutions are practically null for now. Maybe we will see a little hassle out of them on job creation for the rest of economy, and our children.

Analytical Study of Employment Data

Why is there such a big deal about Jobs now, because it is such a big problem? Is it all because of the election? Well perhaps, it is partly about the big election. Otherwise, it is hard to get funds to do the research, and to get the divided attentions to carry out some of the solutions, Still, there are no guarantees, either or both will be carried out. Well, that is enough about high finance of advance research.[8] This graph studies the averages of employment growth rate for all twelve months for 2001 to 2011. This an average recurring pattern, with seasonal explanations.

Figure 9, shows the changes in employment growth rate in different months of the year. That is seasonally from the peak in November and December, which is the charismas gift-shopping season, employment, starts to drop off into April. From April on, the employment starts to increase to the peak of charismas shopping season, again. The months of August and September also show increases. They are back to school and early holidays seasons. February, November, and December show the most growth rates.[9] Now those selected months are studies for their unique characteristics.

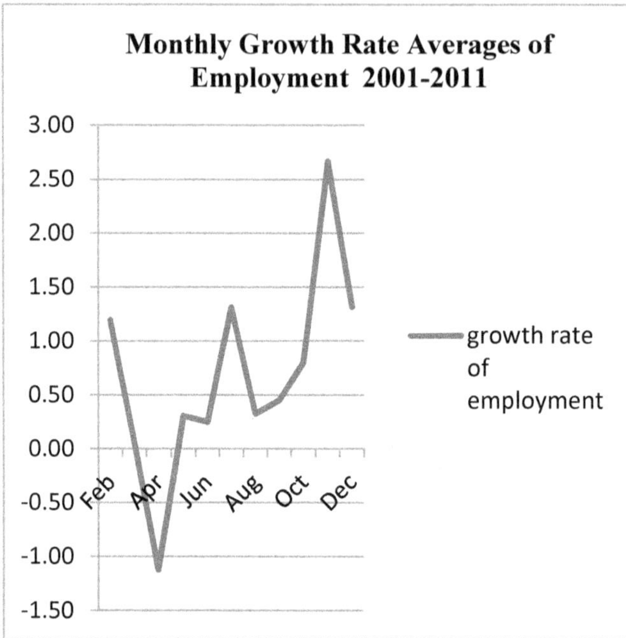

Figure 9, Monthly growth and decay rate of employment averages, for 2001-2011.

April could be the wet season in agricultural term, or job change season in nonfarm terms. Peak of summer jobs and the pre-holidays employment increases can be on that graph.

However, what happens during those good months to employment-rates, over a decade. That question is answered in the next graph.

This will let us know if they have contributively impact data, or there just seasonal influences on the data. Monthly growth rate averages of employment for three selected months of February, November, and December are studies for over the decade of 2001 to 2011. November shows the most peaks in job-creations over those years.

Figure 10 shows total nonfarm employment in thousands for 3-months, over a decade, 2001 to 2011. The specific month spikes points to months which employment rates grow the most.

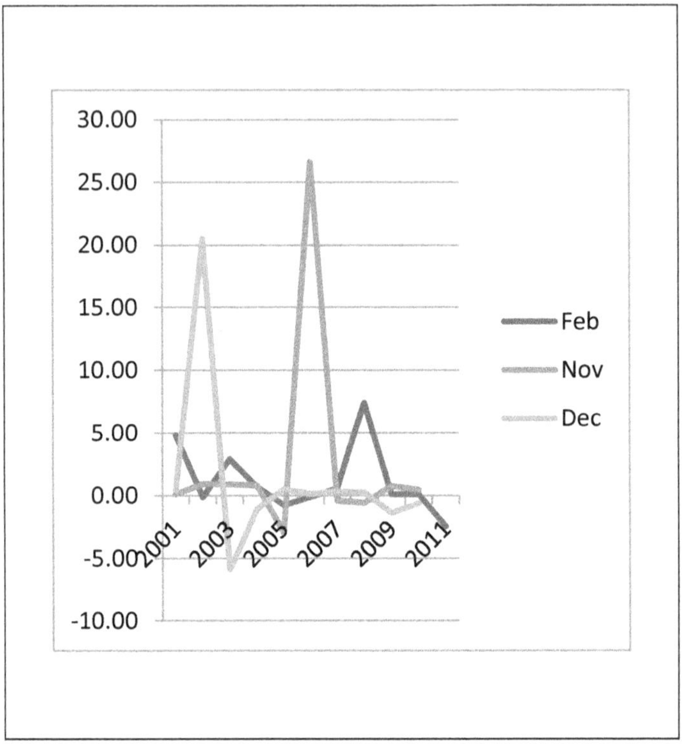

Figure 10, Growth and decay rate of employment for the same months, 2001-2011.

In the following graph, we have changed from rates to total workers employed. Figure 11 shows total nonfarm employment in thousands, for over a decade, 2001 to 2011.[10] The two months of the year show a selected sample, they both ebb and peak mirroring.

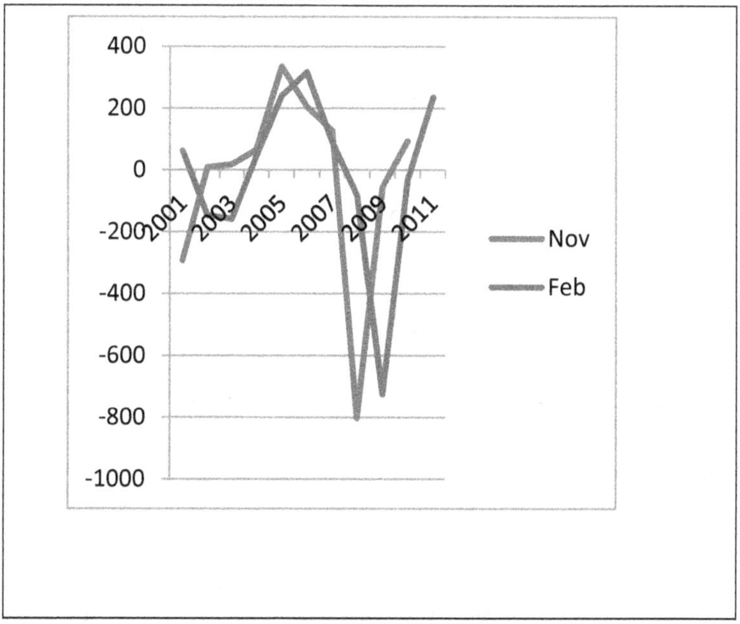

Figure 11, Total numbers of employment for two months from 2001 to 2011.

The total numbers of employments show in the good time we had 400,000 new jobs, but it also shows major economic down turns. Especially when they drop below zero, it shows the severity of the unemployment at below zero negative 800,000 were unemployed after the recent recession in the graph. It is big deep, and looks gruesome, especially for most of us looking for a decent job. The word economic depression is used a lot. Please, remember the 1929-1932 depression dropped in the GDP went passed 30 to 35 percent.

I cannot guarantee that 25 percent unemployment among minority youth, women, and men, in some regions and some countries feels better than that, but there is a huge deference between this last down turn and the 35 percent drop in the economic activity index, the 1930's GDP rates. That is where the government transfers do make a huge difference, the veterans' pay, the social security checks, the disability and unemployment transfers, the Pell grants, the research assistance grants, the federal jobs, all make up the huge difference between todays USA, and a disastrous 35 percent GDP drop depression clausal USA of 1930s.

Therefore, the reasons why we need to concentrate many coordinated efforts on the job area. Since, the numbers can turn on seasonal, or due to further negative economic trends, robotic and technological displacements, or because of political and military shocks. Scientists, researcher can only ask nicely, most of the times, however, they cannot promise you there will not be political shoving and pushing, and oh, a few name-callings, negative campaigns, or even recalls, etc.

Notes

[1] Source: World Bank World Development Indicators, International Financial Statistics of the IMF, global Insight, and Oxford Economic Forecasting, as well as estimated and projected values developed by the Economic Research Service all converted to a 2005 base year.
Real historical Gross Domestic Product (GDP) and Growth Rates of GDP for baseline countries/regions (in billions of 2005 dollars) 1969-2009
Updated: 11/02/09

[2] Source: Calculations and graph are attributed to author. (All figures are estimates based on samples—money amounts are in thousands of dollars)
Table 1, Individual Income Tax Returns: Selected Income and Tax Items for Tax Years 1999 – 2009, IRS-Historical DATA

[3]

https://order.proquest.com/OA_HTML/pqdtibeCCtpItmDspRte.jsp,

[4] Bahman Fakhraie "https://order.proquest.com/OA_HTML/pqdtibeCCtpItmDspRte.jsp

[5] http://www.newsweek.com/2011/01/30/america-s-deporter-in-chief.print.html

[6] The New Jim Crow: Mass Incarceration in the Age of Colorblindness, *legal scholar Michelle Alexander writes that many of the gains of the civil rights movement have been undermined by the* Michelle *Alexander: Jim Crow* Still Exists In America : NPR , http://www.npr.org/2012/01/16/145175694/legal-scholar-jim-crow-still-exists-in-america

[7] Martin Luther King III and Richard Trumka, *Alabama's immigration law: Jim Crow revisited,* Special to CNN, updated 11:23 AM EST, Thu November 17, 2011 http://www.cnn.com/2011/11/17/opinion/trumka-king-civil-rights-alabama/index.html

[8] Author calculated the averages and produced the related graph. http://data.bls.gov/timeseries/CES0000000001?output_view=net_1mth

[9] Ibid

[10] Ibid

CHAPTER 4

Policy Implication

Simmer down for Some Good News, now that you must! The QE3, monetarists pushing on the string, is great if there was the fiscal job-creation and the demand to pull as well. The first attempts to overwhelm the depression forces were either very inadequate for the size of global depression II, or they were overwhelmingly blocked and derided, much to the dismay of all taxpayers. Federal Reserve windows should not open for any big (over $10 million cooperation), if they cannot create or show three, percent per annum sustained increase in their employments. Good cooperate citizen already announce such move on their one.[1] What was explained proficiently, in this article, for which I would have given an A to any economic students, and he is taking flaks from the well healed, is the economic reality that we all live in.[2]

That the progressive taxations have been rung out of the United State Tax Codes! This villainous road to perdition (by the way a very good movie classic with the late great Mr. Paul Newman and the very lively Mr. Tom Hanks) was cheaply paved by the representatives for the wetted money interest lobbyists, who have forgotten their offices and manners in disrespecting the presidency, while they drained the national wealth building and the taxpayers.[3] The downside is that capital formation regulation and stabilities will be targeted, instead of the erroneous misadventures in greed.

Few people who should have known better, manipulated laws for capital formation and associated activities for the tax dodgers, cooperation-monopolies, hedge-fund manager artists. The next quotes from the article detailed the compiled IRS data, but, in recent news we have seen the rates as low as 12-14 percent.[4] The 15 percent capital-formation investment activities is a fine rate, when low and middle level income earners use it as an added rung (steps), but if you use it to hide income, wages and billions of earnings for mega cooperation, Hedge-funds, multi-millionaires, and billionaires, you have fallen in for the wrong revenue enhancement codlings.

That is why the middle-class American old and young, with mortgages and student loans, and the working poor are asking for the economic actions. Trust your better angels, it will get ugly when you are looking at it from the other end of your television shows, ask the x-IMF chief, or any honest Catholic priests. Power and wealth make poor shields in choppy ocean of immoralities drenched with madness of the crowds. I am certain the low-level officious government employee in Tunisia that approached the young businessperson, the Executive (CEO) of the street-cart business for his last bribe, would have also ignored such profound wisdom.[5] Therefore, the advice in the article about progressive adjusted, even temporary, modifications is good council.

Expecting sane responses from madness of the crowd had proven to be insanity indeed. A large number of dictators, Some European countries, much of history even before cake party of French anti-plutocracies' revolution, or Mr. Dracula's true saga do not leave us with warm and fuzzy feeling for the future of the current unattended wealth concentrations.

The United States expansive national poverty data and anti-poverty plans, because it was down in such haphazard and cross propose way, perhaps it was down in total ignorance and not by malicious designs or intends, alas here the economy run aground, and here the menders should get to the job at hand. I hope humanity will not need to sink that low again in human history; nevertheless, there are no grantees. The reason and take this to be sound sagely advice, is not because I have had my Omaha steaks well done at the friendly corner cafe. However, I do not see wisdom, in constant tearing down foundational institutions, federal and state education and higher education centers, universities, schools, research and development projects, infrastructures, local banks, small businesses, functional expedited legal immigration arrangements, which have built up lives in any society, but especially in the United States.

Warren Buffet rule and Paul Walker rule are not silver bullet permanent dynamic solutions, they will tell you this first hand, they are repertory after the fact and mild remedies. They are a number of early baby steps, which adjusts the large ship of state off the rocky shores, in stormy weathers to come.

People whom have confused their hate of presidency, as a paved road to becoming elected president are sadly mistaken. They have had explicit thirty-year chance to create jobs, yet, when they have a chance, they have gone hog-wild to defeat the presidency, rather than to offer jobs by political or diplomatic compromises. That unwelcomed abstractionism is what the majority of unemployed, the 25 percent and their families will remember the most.

In these nihilistic political atmospheres, the rich Americans have become the pons of their institutional lobbyists' successes. However, they purchased all of the stone, and all of the fights and stone throwing will be in their glass castles. Those self-aware titans counseling repertory and balancing solutions are honestly giving their historical assessments and appropriate warnings to all of us, who appreciate lives around us, and the few constructional-realists who still want to stay in politics, and confront the nihilistic destructionists[6]. The kind of economic reality and data that is being evolved around us would have representatives holding hands and singing American the beautiful and confronting job-creation in unity.[7] That is not what we see. They are going to their corners, and holding their breath, until they turn blue. There have been many political leaders, academics, and business leader alarmed at the evolutionary disclosures witnessed. Some leaders pointed out, with even more details, the need to withhold campaign-donations, until the nation sees a palpable political interest in domestic focus, and job-creation in United States.[8] The fruits of these "harvests of wrath" will feel very bitter to those clowning for political ends rewards. This future tsunami may show rumblings and modest protests at first, yet a future unplanned, will plan our collective national and international future for us. If we have any historical recollections, in weeds of past greed, we ought to recall the Vietnam War diseconomy and malcontent. Sure, we blame the end-result on hippies. Nevertheless, the lifestyle alterations were shared by all very democratically.

Therefore, the seeds we sew now ought to be of the harvest quality that we ourselves can tolerably live with. Do onto others, as you like done onto you, or to rephrase a biblical quotation, what we do onto others, shall be done onto us, hopefully, not with so much extra interest. Therefore, a national and international fiscal policy of job creation should take some international effort, perhaps as much as military and other financial plans are preoccupying our present mindset.

Considering everyone is in the same leaky great boat, it is not hard to understand good intentions and optimism. Great people, nations, workers, teachers, students do not vanish they overcome and flourish, and they work for their families, for a better life rather than political intrigues. It is extremely disingenuous, to fight the middle-class workers and economically damage them and cause their real income decline for over thirty years, under guises of some obsolete supply side tinkle-down hocus-pocus proposition, even if, that can work under some assumptive good times, after thirty years to four decades we ought to learn it is not working.

The Internal revenue offices should not extend tax credits, tax subsidies, or an audit free pass to the mega cooperation, if they cannot create or show 3 percent per annum sustained increase in their USA employment rates. They ought to propose a minimum cooperate tax rate for the mega cooperation. These people work for the president's office; last, I checked my civic lessons' notes.

Good presidential decries, tramp bad signature-notes, they can also be good for America. There may be a chance to write short and longer tern job-creation wish lists. While the distinguish citizen-representatives are on their vocation seeping tea or drinking the Kool-Aid. Presidents write their longer emergency goal-lists.

- ✓ Fill all administrative offices by graduates and qualified staff, and trainees. Fill federal departments like Education, Treasury, Justice, Commerce, Agricultures, posts by qualified staff or graduates, or new graduates, and trainees.
- ✓ Decree all government, state, land grant universities and colleges to higher qualified graduates, theirs or swaps, before the next big federal checks arrives.
- ✓ When they scream bloody murder, ask them to come back and write a job creation bill, which will

put people to work, and take care of the infrastructure.

- ✓ Veteran only bills are great symbolic mandates, but not sufficient, nor they are funded past election cycles. They are too small to fight alone. Raise all boats, so the veterans will have a fighting chance with public support and backing.
- ✓ Ensure veterans with the same issues meet as political groups, health groups (AAA, etc.), and business network groups.
- ✓ The plans that are tossed, jeered at, mocked with two-year olds' hand-painting signs can move out to campaign basketball courts and the sharper elbows at election time.

I wrote how president LBJ was sand boxed. However, he could have come out swinging, and won! There are no reasons to assume the worst will occur every time.

Despite Jeers or Adulation, Job-Creation

Europeans' political fascinations with extreme right, even after messianic terrorisms by far-right individuals, are cause for further contemplations. One prepends, is it rumination for economic enlightenments, or the unfortunate regurgitation of past nightmares. The suppositions, which blame multiculturalism (mostly Moslem emigrants this time), in otherwise exclusionary and elitists' cultures, neither contributes or assists Islamic scholars in moderation of Islamic radicalism, nor can it curb the implosive peculations, which have increased joblessness and multicultural misfortunes equally. They have the immorality of latent Machiavellianism, and the violence of Uncle Adolf's Menageries; nevertheless, they have no remedies for mass reemployment.

European governments chose expensive and failed but essential macroeconomic experimentalisms and joblessness, which encouraged the far rights' erroneous trite suppositions. Even international derogatory equating of misdeed of all bad characters and Islamic religion is now fashionable by international neo-fascism, ignoring, and multi-media washing their recent pasts and prominent history of confirmed sinners. Leaderships that fear the extreme right will again fail the western world. In time of economic scarcities, which will test or prohibit "beg thy neighbors" dependencies? Thus, financing adventurousness without full benefit of free trades and enhanced commercial-international trades (otherwise, healthy economies) will only encourage prudence of diplomacy over card blanch militarism. Historically, this modesty of intent seems to have been imposed on the leaderships repeatedly.

Even United State will have hard enough time, to shift from war footing into domestic economically and enhanced job-creation. It is amazing how imperceptibly, with a short skip from the haloed high halls of higher education to certain political catacombs Job-creationism retrogrades into theological creationism and long wars. Alas, these echoes are trite, untrue, unconvincing, and displaced.

Deregulation and Economic Externalities

There are negative and positive economic externalities, which command especial personations in most economic activities. They are studied, and are considered, because they often enlighten us of great hidden values positive or negative, in our soundings. They are deterministic to the supply side of manufacturing, production, and job creation, especially if they are imposed harshly, and suddenly. However, we will see the consumer, or demand side of the equation feel the economic costs of those activates, and the negative externalities are felt by the demand side, first, and then they are felt by most of the economy.

Certain deregulations can be more harmful than bad regulation. Deregulation of meat industry can lead to bacterial outbreaks, and death. Deregulation of clean-coal industries can give us cave-ins in our numerous global coalmines and string of death, toxic streams and lake, acid rain, and the same old expedited carbon-over-loads. Relaxed regulation can unchain petroleum deep-water cowboy-drillings, which wasted Southeast food industry, and for years and billions of dollars, yet to be fully and economically studied.

The unhindered nuclear energy industries can shut down and radiate a third to half of another nation for years and trillion dollars, yet to be partially comprehended or researched. The unencumbered natural gas industries can proceed with their deep well fracturing, yet to be chemically and economically researched, or fully disclosed, which can duplicate the deep well version of oil spill disaster on land, or in ocean. Between those two sides, there are dynamically evolving scientific communities, which can measure, mitigate, and some time reverse the negative impacts of the harmful externalities. It is a fine balanced mix, which cannot be bullied.

Currently, we have to take the words of the industry in forms of commercial outtakes for the future of this great nation. Deregulation of investment banking, the cowboy-securitization of mortgage-industries without the jeered consumer protection regulations, and the fought-regulations of derivative industries have done more than BenLadenism, terrorism can do, but they do it internally.

Yet, no one is droned, in any of these white-color crimes in USA or Europe. Mr. Madoff goes without roommates, and poker hands. The justice department can barely keep up with them. Therefore, the suppositions of the executive suites and their paid lobbyists, that it is either Dodge City or full-unemployment, are manufactured eye-manageress of dangerously unpatriotic greedy robots.

The sententious absolutisms' seeds as grow, they will harm the encumber job-creation for political misdeed, they will yield unfortunate shared harvests. It will only add to the other sins of union bashing, low-wage control, discernible capital mobility, and defalcation of national wealth in the recent past. It will multiply the perceptual sins of domestic populism, and out stretch credulities.

All of the fancy commercials about employing millions, when millions are actually unemployed, or clean industries, while southern regions join others covered with a shin of crude oil will not dissuade harsh observations. Especially if they are untrue, they will finally bring exacting regulations, after alerted customer, citizens, elect only less-friendly representatives. Their purchase price will exceed their worst to the judgments of major owners and shareholders. The following shows income taxes collected by type.[9] Figure 12 shows tax collections for business income and individual income taxes, 1960-2010.

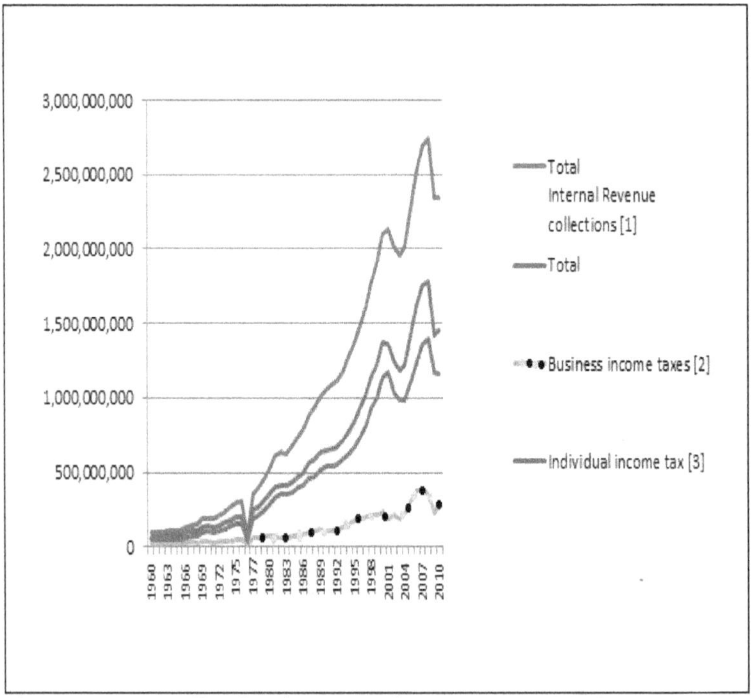

Figure 6, Tax collection by type of taxes, 1960-2010.

In addition to the shape of the graphs above, the econometrical analysis of the magnitude of slope of growth rates, show three important points.

$$\frac{\partial T}{\partial I_t} \geq \Omega 1 \quad \frac{\partial T}{\partial B_t} \geq \Omega 2$$

One is the positive direction of increases. However, what is alarming, is not only the difference, largeness of sigma one, over sigma two, but the rate of taxation in sigma one. It shows that more is extorted than received by individuals under the current system. That is what has been unsustainable for some time.

$$\Omega 1 \approx 1.02 \quad \Omega 2 \approx 0.77$$

Therefore, the cogent solutions incognizance in these complex arithmetic of taxation-rates analyses of statistical slope of growth rate of actual collections, and from different classifications by IRS are also yielding adventitious answers.

Unfortunately, for the nescience political party, increasing fees and further taxes on the larger sigma will prove counterproductive. Job-creations will increase the bases, but the quality of the jobs, and take-home incomes are the determinant policy jolt.

Especially, it becomes hypocritical, when they have deemed the lower sigma a job killer repeatedly. That is why the insistence that immigration law modification had been urged incessantly away from the populous emotionalism nature of the 1996 alteration to that law. Because simply halving sigma one will not be accomplished by nativist sentimentality. That is even after full employment policy implementation of government job for all PhDs including, liberal arts graduates, besides getting a speed in the no-hassle multiple fees citizenship-queue that goes on for years.

The nature of population declines and the baby-boomers' population-spikes have been dynamic econometrics' composition certainties, they are deterministic of all economic activities. Moreover, the CEO wages, bonuses, and looting fiascos are simply not sufficient to widen and deepen the base revenues. Moreover, the fraudulently set tax rate too low for the billionaires and too high against the middle class will not bring any more revenue.

Manufacturing in particular domestic manufacturing requires an educational expansion, retraining goals. Then the invention, innovational, and capital formation require a fermentation time elements no sooner than five to ten years, if private investors, entrepreneurial capitals were not bitten and now totally too shy to venture domestically.

The very dysfunctional immigration law system has done serious damage to the inner structural working of the

USA capitalist system. The once mutually gainful relationship of the legal immigrants, their trusts, and their investment requirements have been deliberately hacked to death. By some very peculiarly xenophobic-regurgitated notions, that now surfaces among some political dilatants, some seriously disturbed governors, and radical political party hacks.

The "self-deportation," comment like the self-guilt of the self-genocides of the certain Japanese citizens' campgrounds had a cleansed distasteful sound to it, as passage of time divulged that it was not a ill and fully demented joke.

These ideas of criminally violating civil and constitutional rights of real Americans by Olympic size moochers and southern strategists are amazingly self-destructive. These are pathetic death claws and finger wagging of nihilistically condemned hate-groups that have body-snatched the GOP. If this keeps up, even the late comers will have to apologies for the GOP, before saving it, from the underfoot muck of barnyard abstractionisms. What is standard practicing these days was not the practice of polite society even in the dark days of American retrogressions, far away from legitimate and intellectually honest, lighthouse on the hill ideals of great Americanisms, or even average human decencies of most American people.

Therefore, we have to go back to the one good idea that they wrecked the domestically productive housing industry. The only short-term reparatory constructive, domestically contained economic activity, which had, and will employ the most Americans in America, was and still is, and will be domestic housing industries.

Financiers will go bust, and blame the economists, who warned them, just to hide those facts. Mega bankers will lay mega-eggs. People on the boob tube will hauler. Bondholders and hedge fund managers will have to pay real taxes at real rates like everyone else at 35 percent! Nevertheless, until and unless federal reserve bank prints money and causes an inflationary pressure, and jobs and infrastructural reconstruction picks up, and real disposable income increases, and prices and housing price increase, the economy stays slow for ten years cycles.

The true and certain data that has exacted economic events in modern USA millennial economy is the growth and decay rates of population and the millennial economic activities, the USA economy. Mainly, population data shows the increase or decrease in such economic activities. Figure 13 shows the rate of declines in the population, from 1991-2010.[10]

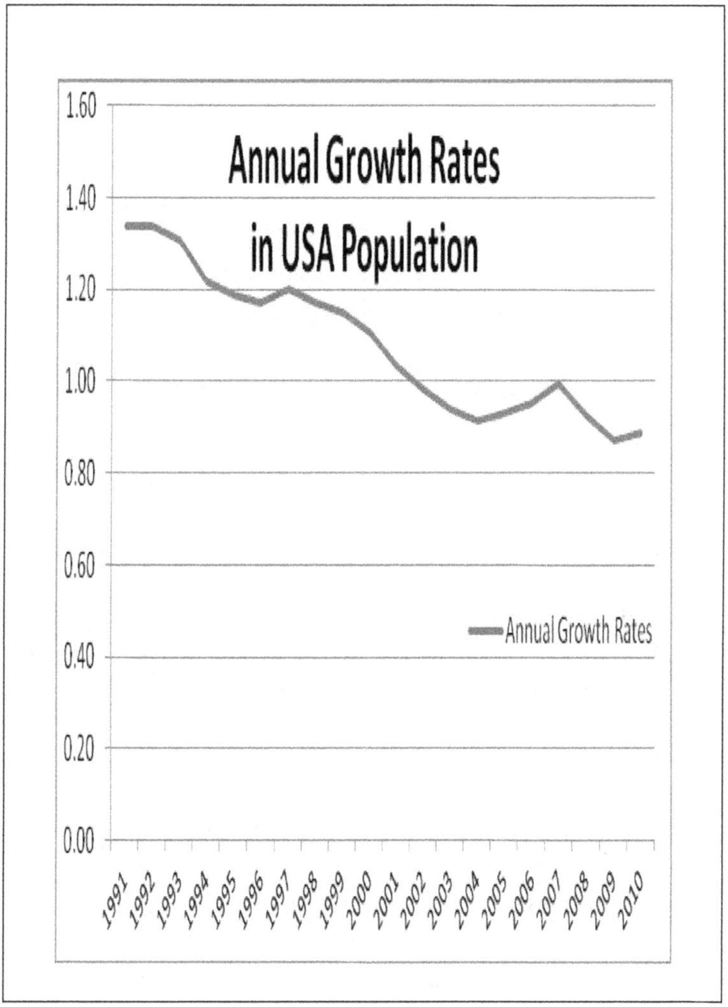

Figure 13, Annual growth and decay rate of population, USA, 1991-2010.

Therefore, take the new normal, put it in your funny pipes, and smoke it.[11] Until you see, my friends' double visions of cheap genus and the notion of above average become one vision for you. If you keep overcharging for health, then keep sucking at the hookah, and make sure the charcoals are hot. Smoking is still bad for your health, so we will need the universal health care.

There have been some Ponzi schemes and some Al Capone angles, and now we find out they will not even pay their fair tax shares to fix the country, which they get to enjoy the most.

The lowest green graph shows how much the business paid versus the individual income taxes, total income taxes paid, and total revenue collated by IRS. Nevertheless, American middle class, elderlies, students and their mega student loans ($30 to $300 thousands), academics, teachers, firefighters, policepersons, and legal immigrants are the victims of these destabilizing speculations, as the political onionskins peel off these rotting-political party two-step shuffles. Americans are discovering the real perpetrators of the heinous unpatriotic greed and cash-hording for the new millennium, the patriot acts I, II, FISA laws were not for them.

They live on the hill. They do not want to pay their fair share of taxes, which maintains the colored-glassed cathedrals on those hills. Worst yet, they ignore sage consul. The few percentage adjustments in your mega billions will not harm but benefit the country, and the economy, if it goes toward true job-creation, and the sustainable economic model, rather than your private wealth creation agendas.

The figure 14 shows growth and decay rate of profit, wages, and salaries as percentage of gross domestic product.[12]

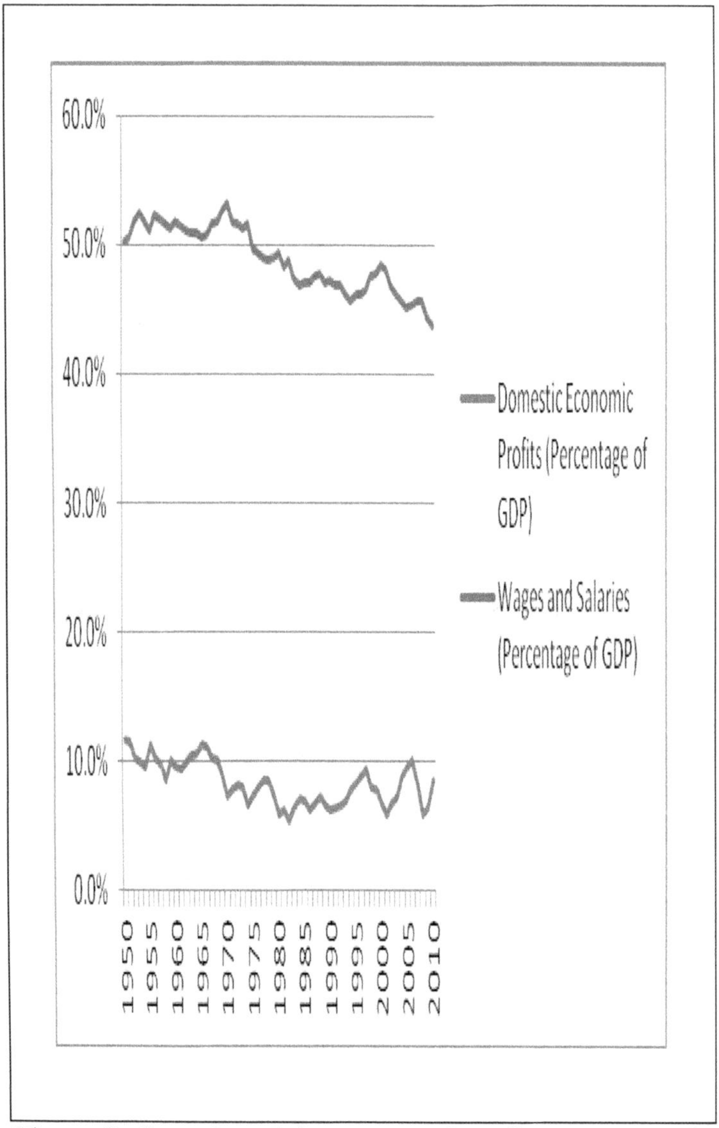

Figure 7, Growth and decay rate of profits, wages, and salaries as percentage of GDP.

Since 1970s, the declines in growth rate of population and wages, and profit as percent of economy are prominent. Moreover, math will tell us the 10 percent of the economy alone cannot master job-creation that the 55 percent of the economy did in the good old days, government is part of this deductive job-creation solution. However, paying their share is a good start. Why is it, the 10 percent get all the resources of the republic tied up in their beneficial lobbyists' clouds.

The following is the statistical averages of monthly growth rate of employment in United States for over a decade.[13] This also shows seasonal tendencies useful to remember in most economic and political cycles' forecasting. Figure 15 shows three months are particularly important in election cycles. They are not all above zero. They are runway trains independently.

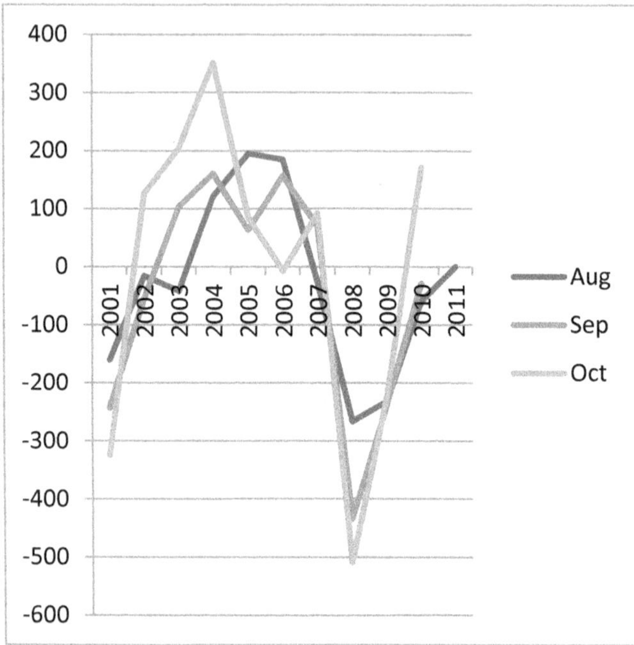

Figure 8, Growth and decay employment rates for 3-months averages, 2001-2011

We are supposed to shut off the 2.5 million-government job engines meekly in a bad prolonged recession, while cooperation hoarded profits and cash, and discernibly lumbered 1.5 million temp-type work and Mac-jobs, excluding the executive bonus bundles.

This would have been much easier, if demand side technological injections were much larger and were aimed at domestic nondefense expansions, it went to TARP one (the save the investment bankers fund, the American version, and then the European version), and over the table defense and under the table defense, the mushrooming and unaccountable security concrete.

So, we do not know other than the few people that touch your junks in airport, are there job-creations or criminal frauds under the security acts, or cash transfers in airports of Baghdad and Kabul? Even thou, they claim they did not see more than 2 or 3 million dollars in roads and buildings in these countries! However, certain political party has had ample times to play abstractionisms, abandonments, denial and blame, insider trading, catcalls and jeers, along with their new "do-nothing religion absolutions."

The next graph shows growth rates for groups of nations in the global economy. Most economic book on international trade, tell us that international commerce kicks in to buy American goods, or inject capital human and financial capita in our economy in bad times, that is what keep employment, disposable real incomes high and money velocity higher in trading economies. That is that we will bring the economy out of the economic down turns, and the executives can charge whatever they want. That was the old model. The other economies have to be growing, with disposable real income of their own. The trend line of economic activities in these different groups of nation tells us about the interdependencies, which binds us all to the same faith. Therefore, the new trade model will tell us the same exact same thing, if only other economies were functioning properly. One aspect of tumultuous and dynamic economic and political restarting, and in light of modern technological innovations in multimedia, and instantaneous communications, beside the interjected uncertainties, are the potential for expansions of commerce, cross-cultural exchanges, and none defense trade. The road maps how to get there, often starts with their embryonic democracies to become functional bifurcated political parties, which will let go of the 10-20 percent operating capacity economies that become inclusive of minorities. Moreover, they ought to get off the war-megalomaniacs' merry-go-arounds. Figure 16 shows four decades trend line rate of decay in real rate of growth of Gross National products (r gdp rates) in different groups of nations.

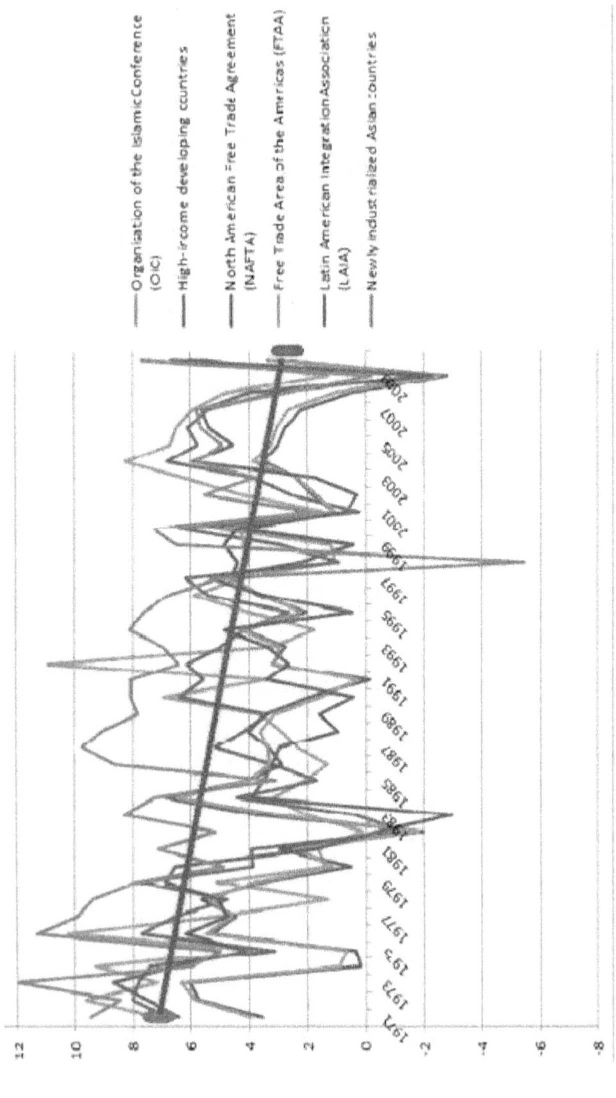

Figure 9 : Growth and decay rates real GDP for groups of nations, 1971-2010.

The four decades trend line decay is not an arithmetic mirage, or an error margin, or a temporary outlier that has gotten away from the Teconometricians.[14] It has the royal regalia of structural permanency chiseled all over it. This graph alone ought to convince you to look at the cross elasticity of economic prosperity across the borders, "If you break it, you will really pay for it."

All these time small businesses were snookered out of capital market, and the middle class are bamboozled out of the payroll tax breaks to boost aggregate demand temporarily. Remember that social security number check President Bush sent you 2001, that is that peak in 2002-2003 in the above graph. Why are they squabbling about another boost to the middle-class? Why the stimulus was halved for this president? With the structural unemployment so high, and infrastructural projects ignored, why are they hollering deficit? This latent riotousness of reformed perennial deficit-spending sinners is cheap political theater for their well-coddled meal tickets and your votes.

Broken Political-Economic Models.

Hence, we start over with another true job-creation plan amongst the jeers, instead of adulations. We have more economic tools to deal with inflations, but sparse few tools to deal with stagflations. The American infrastructures, unlike the mushrooming security buildings, are fading away in neglect, pancaking roads and bridges, imploding-waterways undergrounds, and the disemboweled schools. Teachers, educators, parents with declining real disposable incomes, which cannot afford to put the children through the postgraduate higher education. These entire infrastructures and more, the employment of teachers and professors, they want the America to languish with quotidian joblessness, while they amass thirty more silver and gold coins! Here are domestic wolves, sharks, and DC-BenLadenism we can no longer effort.

There are at least two distinct system models, which can be functional. One is a functional but recursive very negative model, an exclusionary implosive model, which cannot internalize external shocks, and rejects population waves, which the economy depends on to grow and stay functional, this model did very well in the old-world that was historically (under natural or forced) homogeneity. These systems will have a very bad time in the globalized modern economies with increasing heterogeneity. They become unsustainable models.

<u>And Sustainability</u>

The second system model is Model two, it is an adoptive inclusive dynamic model. These systems do better with modern socioeconomic shocks, like population wave-shocks. They can normally internalize and digest smaller shocks. They are more sustainable. Nevertheless, when they become dysfunctional, xenophobic, or anti-social, they do not adjust readily to socioeconomic and political shocks, and they will implode with joblessness, and unrests. They are not sustainable system models.

American people as people around the globe have too many shared lives, their familial, friendly and commerce connections to succumb to depression of efforts and smallness of bad intentions, and illiberal narrowness of minds. The real GDP growth rate graph shows a number of economies that have sustained economic growth rates between 2 to 6 percent. Therefore, it is not an oddity to want to improve United States economy to its potential capabilities.

That is, that didactic poetry, which the madness of far rights cannot comprehend about legal immigration, about freedom that all people seek. The scientific wholeness and modernity of positivism seeded in the modern functional communities, which multiculturalism has cultivated even outside academic high halls.

People will know, not to trust the same power drunk, tax the poor and middle-class crews, with their economic lives, again. Not unless, they are sure, they are well away from the depression ledges, that the political party led them there, and left them there, not long ago. You ought not to be able to fool all of the people, all of time. It is unnatural, and yes counter intellectual, unscientific, even illiberal. Moreover, the hypocrisy and the unintellectual contortions are painful to all constituencies, which suffer from the negligence of these parties "irreligious absolutions." We sure have not seen signs of intellectual economic lives among the other political party, despite the full-time alien probing, by media. In presence of intellectual candidate, they immediately retrograde to their designated underground intellectual man caves.

In a functioning democracy, the demonstrated infelicitousness of empathy will invite the luscious victory of the other party, unfortunately after some two years more languishing of real 10 to 25 percent unemployed and underemployed, and some 60 to 80 percent upset constituencies? We can even go back for the old fashion 6 month of nasty useless squabbling, called "election campaigns television season" to enrich the media Inc. The current political economic model of election has failed the nation. First Amendments' right does not explain the monopolizations of time and human capital resources of the democracy for personal gain of reelection.

Permanent electioneering dominates the mind and resources of the elected, and those wishing to be reelected, without stiff regulation and limitation of such related activities to two limited periods, prior to democratic elections, for both primary and final election requirement.

Henceforth, for the betterment of America, job-creation we must! President Ronald Reagan did not let the business sector to forget their obligations, but they did forget repeatedly. Therefore, he enacted new taxes some eleven times to remind them of their duties. Do not let them forget it. When president Obama reminds them of their recent bail out, their paid voices scream socialism.[15]

> "But we need to meet the moment. We've got to up our game. We need to remember that we can only do that together. It starts by making education a national mission — a national mission. Government and businesses, parents and citizens. In this economy, a higher education is the surest route to the middle class. The unemployment rate for Americans with a college degree or more is about half the national average. And their incomes are twice as high as those who don't have a high school diploma. Which means we shouldn't be laying off good teachers right now -- we should be hiring them. We shouldn't be expecting less of our schools -- we should be demanding more. We shouldn't be making it harder to afford college -- we should be a country where everyone has a

chance to go and doesn't rack up $100,000 of debt just because they went."

They like to forget that the bulk of stimulus funding was spent on them. It was misallocated to them to save them, in a vein hope they will loan out and aid the job creation. However, when it came time for infrastructure construction, teacher and professors' employments and pay adjustments, the real motive became defeatism, abstractionism, and the do-nothing nihilistically dysfunctional party politics.

It was not saving the American economy, employing the taxpayers and job creation, raising their real income, improving the national revenue and income, resurrecting the middle class, or protecting and easing your voting rights. It will serve you well to remember that in the verbalism of 2012 election, and in the hallowed voting cubical. That is the royal majesty of the constitutional rights gives you all Americans. If you think, they have not tried mightily to narrow it, limit it, fee it, redistrict it, or take it away you have not read your own history.

Modern Problems and Solutions

Application of Game Theory has found new students in applied econometrics and some social sciences are catching up to us. That is the way of science. The methodology was applied to early 1980s-1990s to western economic and political economy, after using it on my thesis in technological change and economic growth theory and social welfare economic.

In this shorter study, figure 17 shows the empirical data of global gross national product growth rates. That is compared with the western economies selected unemployment indices for youth, and others.

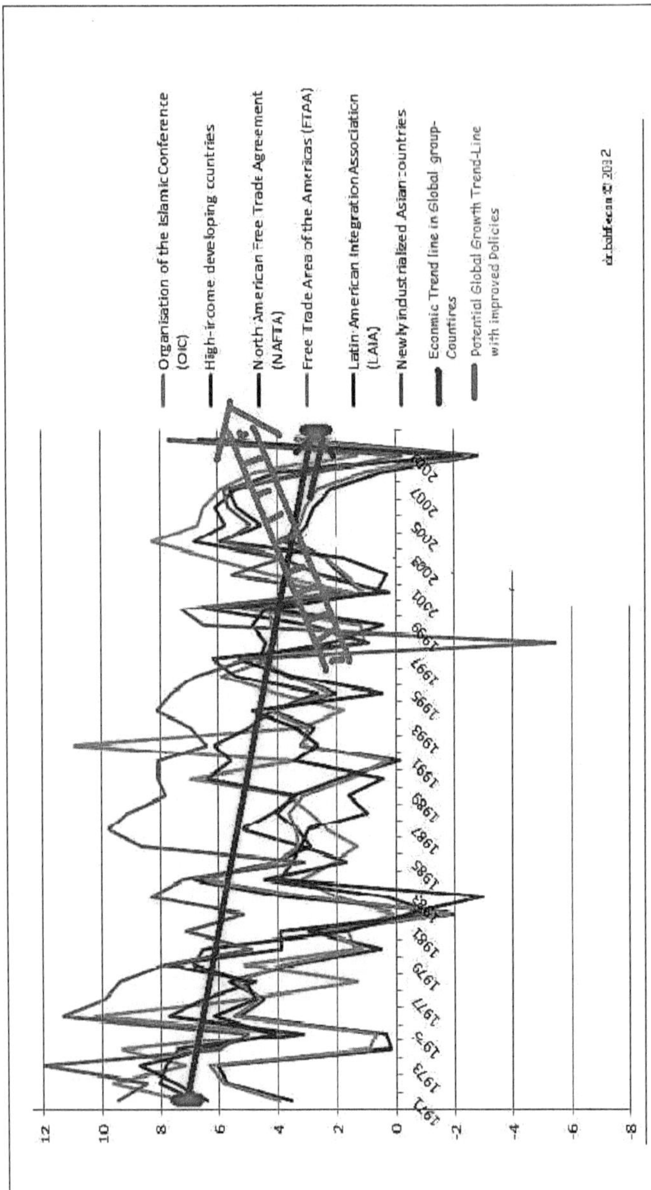

Figure 10 , Average growth and decay rates in real GDP for groups of nations,1971-2010.

The more recent youth data reflects the same issues, which earlier minority and youth data.[16] Related to minorities and less represented elements of these economies, and study the correlation of their incidences of general social unrest in the same economies relative to each other.

The hypotheses of global connectivity in culture have long been accepted. International instant links and connectivity, with or without assists has flourished and confounded control freaks globally. Benladenisms, other terrorism, many versions of Western neo-fascisms, and anti-multiculturalism have been so overwhelmed they have gone apoplectic and vindictive. Some theological movements may join them. However, global commerce had not waited for governance or guidance. That has unhinged many psychics as well.

Even those societies, which knew how to plan, have been overwhelmed, because, the technological injections have been so massive and powerful and fast. Traditional cultures and Westerns, and eastern cultures alike need to rethink, retrain, and come together, in order to find a calm path through these storms. The implication of trends of declines, unemployment, and societal unrests are not very positive, unaltered. In modern conflicts, there are too much waist and capital destructions, which may prove fatal to all, and not just onside, or the other. What the trend line in figure 11 explains, the unemployment data reemphasizes. The only unifying logic here is that we all need to grow, and commerce economic growth, is the only way out. How we entangled it matters, but only by degrees, when all economies need to resources, employments, and growth. Figure 12 shows more recent Europeans' youth unemployment data.

Europe Youth unemployment

Austria	8.2
Germany	9.1
Denmark	12.3
Malta	12.3
Luxembou	13.3
CzechRpb	16.7
Belgium	18.3
Slovenia	18.4
Cyprus	19.6
U. Kingdo	19.6
Finland	19.9
Estonia4)	20.4
France	22.8
Rumania	22.8
Sweden	23.1
Poland	23.6
Hungary	24.8
Portugal	26.8
Ireland	26.9
Bulgaria	27.3
Italy	27.8
Latvia4)	29.7
Lithuania	32.6
Slovakia	33.3
Greece	38.5
Spain	45.7
eu avgs	25

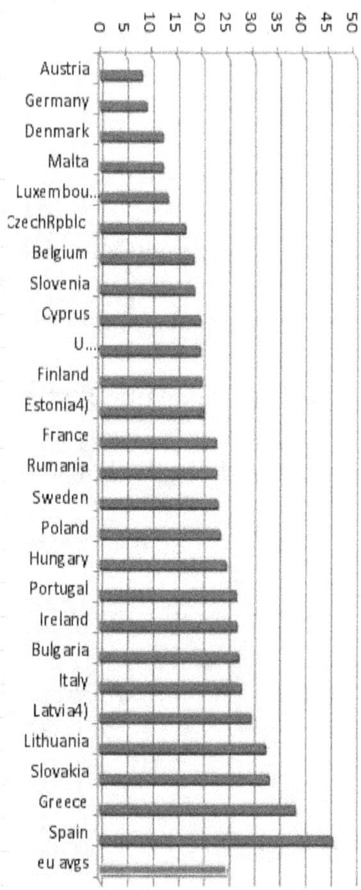

Figure 11; European youth unemployment 2012 data.

The conclusion is not too difficult to ascertain, when the graphs are studies. What is more important is what each culture has designed to remedy the difficulties these complexities present. The very old European strategies has also been tried by others around the globe, blaming the underdogs, genocidal eradication policies, and exporting the problems have dangerous consequences, which even militarisms will not remedy now. Those good old strategies of burning the house down to get rid of the fleas are as stupid now as they were then, capital destruction is an economic minus, and it is not a financial externality plus, regardless of the spin. They have to be complementary constructive policies to create jobs, and rebuild these societies. Let us, do better. We are all able to do better now.

1. Fake assimilation to cheat the unknowing feigners only delays and compounds the negative results. It

interjects mistrusts, especially, when their human and other capital-investments, entrepreneurship and endless energy have proven to be historically deterministic to dynamic successes of modern economies.

2. Resource striping them at home and cheating them out of employment at home and abroad will have definite economic complications. One of which is no adequate demand in a competitive condition facing other products-differentiated supply economies. Another one problem is the continual supply of workers tax revenues, and social security revenues for baby boomers, as age composition dictates economic realities.
3. Undoing other democracies will grantee you some non-democratic hostile alternatives, you will not

like to deal with and they will not like to deal with you, without paying higher externality margins.

4. Torturing and border transgressions do not look good when dictators do them. It will not look good when democracies bamboozle themselves into doing them. Even, if UN words or gestures are manipulated to supply guarded veils of indecencies.

Militarisms have an inescapable self-terminating economic retrogression to it. They also have self-perpetuating monopolistic tendencies internally, which will corrupt the competitively perfected market economies. The finality of it is economically self-terminating, recursive. Either you have an exit plan at the start, or one will be handed to you with your head at the exit, with the blood of innocence to remind you and them. That would hardly induce international commerce with democratic options. Alternatively, that will not encourage sound rational dynamic endorsements of reciprocity and free trade in competitive markets, as short-term remedy. So doing the right thing, is not a new Politically correct wisdom handed to you in a Chayi khaneh free, or psycho bobbles in Western liberal schools. It has the power and logic of mathematical theories behind it. Nevertheless, you do as you please, as your supremacists' past dictates to you and take the consequences on the hard.

Unconstitutional Victimizations Laws and the States' Decaying Economies are a volatile mix. It is a point of law that Conspiracy to engage in anti-constitutional actions by state authorities by legislators or law enforcements are also against the law. It becomes a common practice, with the mindset of ignorance and xenophobic bigotry. In some states, it is a common practice to vote unconstitutional laws and resend them as matter of common business. It is busy work to fool hometown hicks, unless the bad laws remain on the books.

Figure 19shows unemployment of male youth natives and none natives. Figure 20 shows stability issues.

We stipulate the data from the following source, "From president's economic report 2004" shows the unemployment percentages of adults and youth.

Adult (foreign, native), youth (foreign, native)

France: 30+17+17+7=	71
Sweden: 23+9+16+6=	54
Spain,	44
UK: 14+11+10+6=	41
Germany:12+7+13+7=	39
Canada,	30
USA	29
Australia	28
Japan	27
Netherland	19

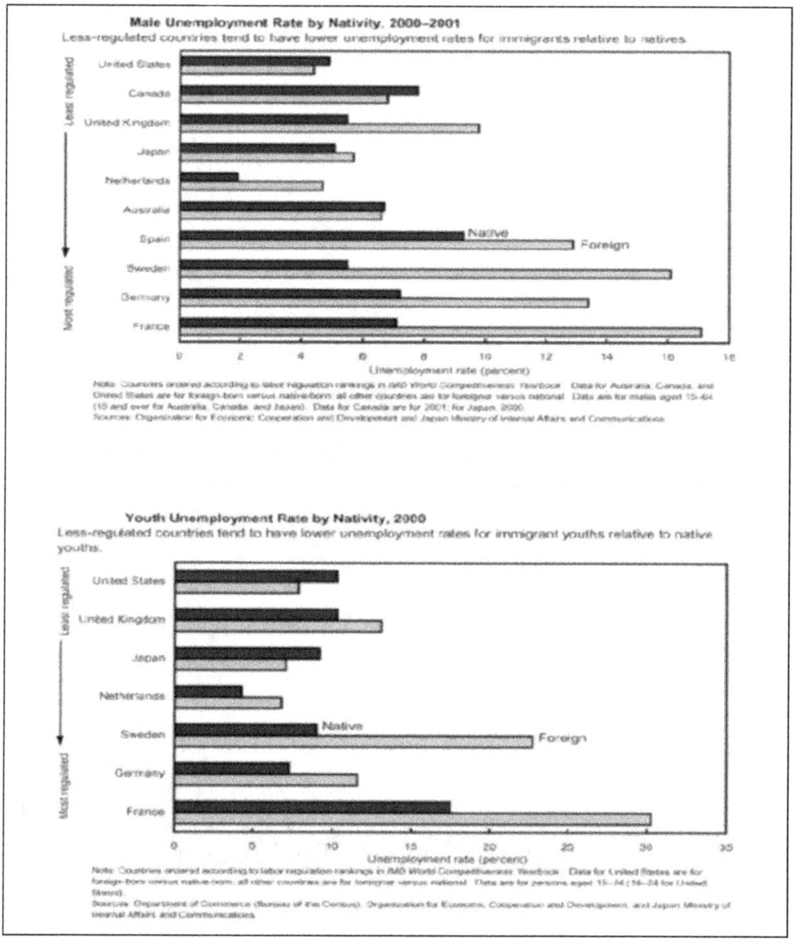

Figure 12, Male and youth unemployment by nativity 2000-2001.

Figure 13, shows the Policy matrix for constructive trends.

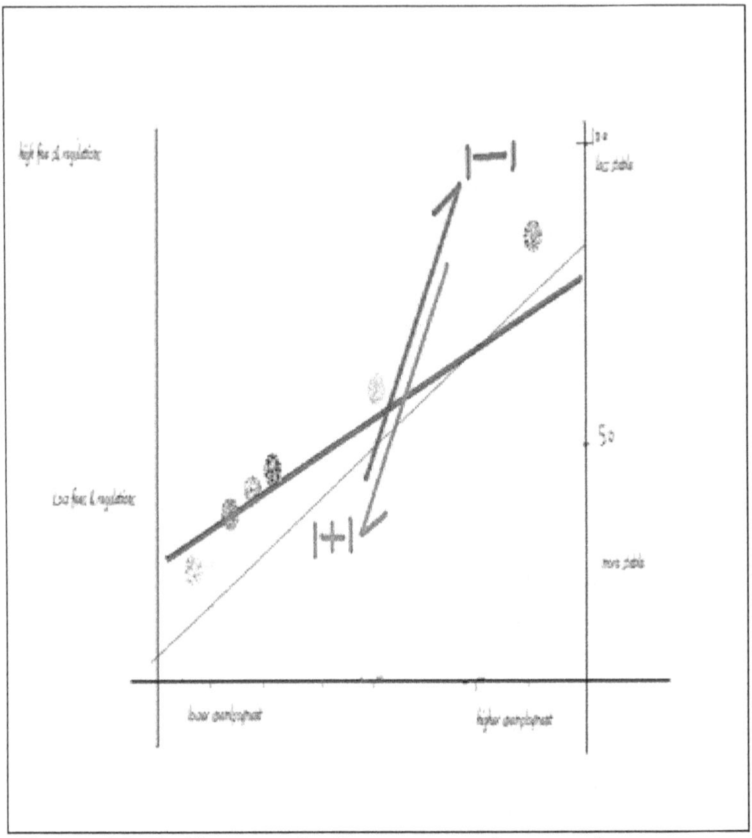

Figure 13, Policy matrix for constructive trends

Reducing fees and streamlining appropriate regulations, increasing employment adds to the stability and more rational discourse. Unfortunately, exclusionary legislations have been misused nihilistically to harm. Figure 14 uses Bayesian decision matrices.

<table>
<tr><td></td><td>low
unemployment
Gov-assists+
Job-retraining</td><td>high
unemployment
Gov-assists?-
No job-
retraining</td><td>Less barrier to
Free & fair
trade
Allowing
mobility
of workers and
CAPITAL</td></tr>
<tr><td>Lower fees
and
abstractive
none
inclusive
laws,
Inclusive</td><td>< 20%</td><td>50-70%</td><td rowspan="2">BDMI >50%
Requires
Intervention
Gov. policies
to reduce it.
****
BDMI<50
Requires
private
Ngo assists
To further
stabilize.
****
Job creation
Fees-
performance
Realignments,
Law reviews,
Non-alienation
Reviews,
Modernizations,
Ed.& job access</td></tr>
<tr><td>High fees
And
exclusive
Punitive
Regulations
Exclusive</td><td>20-50%</td><td>70-100%</td></tr>
<tr><td>Dangerous
politics,
Bigoted-
xenophobic
/exclusionary
racer bating
victimizing
policies</td><td>More
Stable
Less costs
Sustainable</td><td>Less
Stable
More costs
Unsustainable</td><td>Policy
modification
required
Anti racism
Anti
xenophobic
Exclusionary-
anti education</td></tr>
</table>

Figure 14, Using Bayesian decision matrix indices.

Some of the extreme legislations are like explaining the hangmen-nose events as positive expression of free speech amendment! Some higher education employers tried that logic on me a few years back. These are anti-intellectual cross burnings in immigrants and poor minorities' backyards both. This is the tail-tell of Stalinist' institutionalisms, the xenophobic bigots with failed smelly tortured intellects. These are no solution polemics and tautological mind benders, which walk you into the quicksand of social unrests, and keep you there a few decades.

The Education and Honest Capital Formation

Since 1970s, we have been told the education matters, research is the future of the country, what we put in education we get 3 times back. That part is true. The next part is not true, or the collective-judgments have become foggy. That the governments of United States with the Europeans and other advanced economies have refocused all effort in education to boost (not boast) the national wealth with the wisdom of their crowds upward, and increase their level of livings, such that raising tides lifts all boats.[17] Moreover, there has been a dedicated millennial plan to refocus on more funding and higher education to pull up the global economies into a more prosperous and less trouble place. That is not reflected in the data.

Figure 15, shows market consolidation of USA investment banks in the last few decades. The financial crisis of 1980s, and 1990s were endogenously formulated.[18] Endure. Figure 15 also explains the larger mega-investment banks influence capital formation and will remain consequential to circularity of money supplies, and economic cycles, they will be revisited.

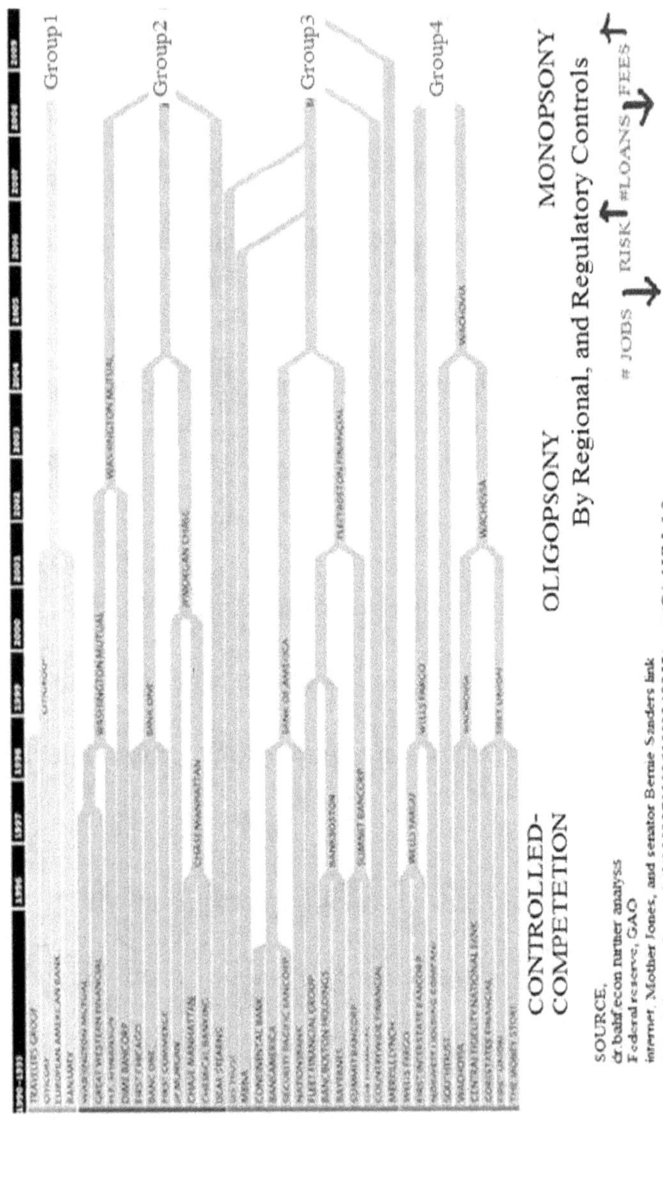

Figure 15. Market and price implication of restructure of USA investment banks.

Events increased the risk of banks holding mortgages securitization, security derivatives, and swaps related to mortgages.[19] When the market prices turned, the regulators arrangements reduced the number of big investment banks. There are larger numbers of regional banks, and they may

There are fewer big banks, which influence services, fees, numbers of loans, and number of jobs created.[20] Therefore, too big to fail and middleclass, main street bail out of risky behaviors are also with us. Hence, the size of future TARP-n will make the repetition of the policy cost-prohibitive. Nevertheless, the levels of risks in different institutions are different.

This next concept is followed religiously by to international students and American and European student alike, but is it true? Moreover, the prejudices of uneducated world and not in the "educate world," easily undermines gradual and incremental rewards, which are supposed to be there.

The data samples are too limited and much more resources are required to develop this in an acceptable academic work, but the result from multiple confirmation sources point at it strongly. If NSF funding of research project proven vaporous or mercurial, so will the statistical study and results.[21] Yet, the regression analysis of a very limited data and statistical quality still points out that the rewards of qualified (quality) education are positive.[22]

Figure 16 shows us income per capita for 2006 in ranked metropolitan locations.

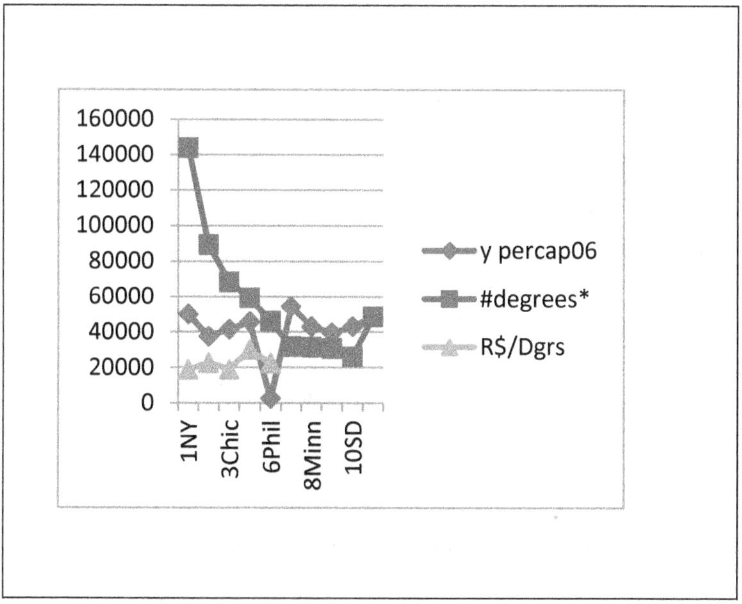

Figure 16, Income per capita, degrees, and research fund per degree in ranked metros.

It also shows the dollars of research spend per degrees in research fund in the same areas. The estimated average income per capita of metropolitans' centers in Untied States reflected the rest of data, that they are uniformly bellow $60000, however the other interesting numbers is the graph about research dollar funded to degreed individuals, in these metropolitans are very minimal. Those numbers will have to improve to reflect the bombast of political promises, and match the real hours of present needs. Right wing nuts, anti-education groups, political demagogues develop television commercials about people become millionaires, watching grasshoppers or shrimp procreate, as the perverted version of welfare-mom millionaires with Lincoln continentals. That is not true. Yet, the CEO's private jets, and cooperate welfares, which are true. Those just make us want to believe intuitively the commercials of them pushing the grandma off the Medicare, healthcare, and social security ledges, instead of job creation, revenue enhancements, and true solutions.

The econometrics of the data analysis even with the very limited data sample, divulges a few nuggets. The slope of linear regression of income per capita for 2006 and numbers of degrees for the metropolitans are positive numbers. That is about 66 percent higher than the slope of linear regression of income per capital and research funded dollars per degrees in the same metro areas. The better data sample shows a better statistic. The linear regression number between income per capital and degrees are 42 times higher, than the other two slopes. It is 2.10, that is a $1 invested in a degree generate $ 2.10 in income per capita in metro area of this econometric analysis, with limited samples.

That was the logic behind the proper student loan strategy to rebuilt human capital. That like the mortgages, housing, and fixed capital was criminally corrupted, into payola and payday mechanism to fill the tax break deficits, high jacked to benefit the top 1 percent. Until, the NSF or other funding materialized for a decent researcher and a longer-term research, we can assume the students were bamboozled. It went the same way as for the fixed capital mortgage holders. For those student loan recipients since 1999, which were bamboozled with 3 percent come-on rates, either the students have to be employed by the government mandate, or their student loans ought to be studied to be forgiven write-downs. The deficit holes need to be refilled by the adjustments in the 15 percent tax rates of hedge funds and money managers, instead of their true 35% rates, and other tax credit breaks of the billionaires and the 1 percent top income earners. They should fund the decent researchers' studies as well, to remedy the economic damages they have caused.

One way to study where the growth of income has been spent since 1930s, is to analyze the income cross elasticity of changes in growth of different sectors of nation income account relative to growth rate of gross national product. [23] That is, more than one percent growth in each sector has to come from their share in one percent growth of GDP, or by internal or external borrowings, or temporal changes in future revenues. Only proper investments have the temporal revenue increase options. Capital formation (human, and tangibles), are the kind of investments, which can include technological injections, and innovational expansions.

Education, production units like, in factories (Ford, Chrysler, Chevy, Agro, techno, Industries, etc.) have that capabilities.

Figure 17 studies the change in rate of growth of consumption, investment, and national defense, per one percent change in growth of GDP 1930-2006.

While the relative change in investment stays around 1 percent, the consumption increases from 1.7 to over 2 percent estimated.

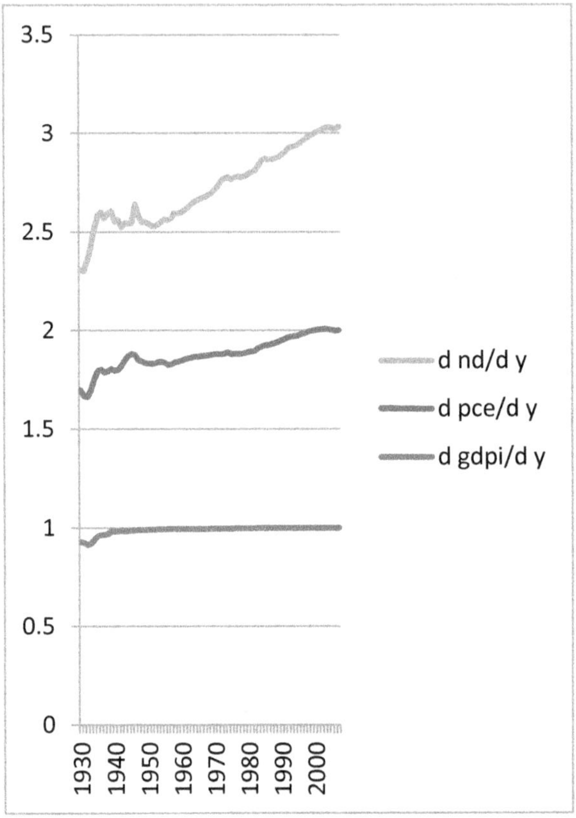

Figure 17, Elasticity of rate of growth for selected variable per 1 percent growth of GDP.

However, the growth in income elasticity of national defense expenditures starts from 2.3 and goes to 3 percent, for the same period. World War Two only managed to show a blip, (2.5-2.7 percent) around 1946, then the increase accelerates after 1960s (2.6-3.1 percent). For a growth-oriented economy, theoretically, the incomes cross elasticity of investment and consumption should top the graph, which then finances the other sectors (military consumptive expenditures), because what you are investing in matters.[24] Otherwise, the dynamic differences are paid out of deficits and borrowings.[25]

Figure 18, shows the index ratio of gross fixed capital formation to nominal gross national product.[26] The data is reflecting recent post-crash economic activities, in the United States.[27]

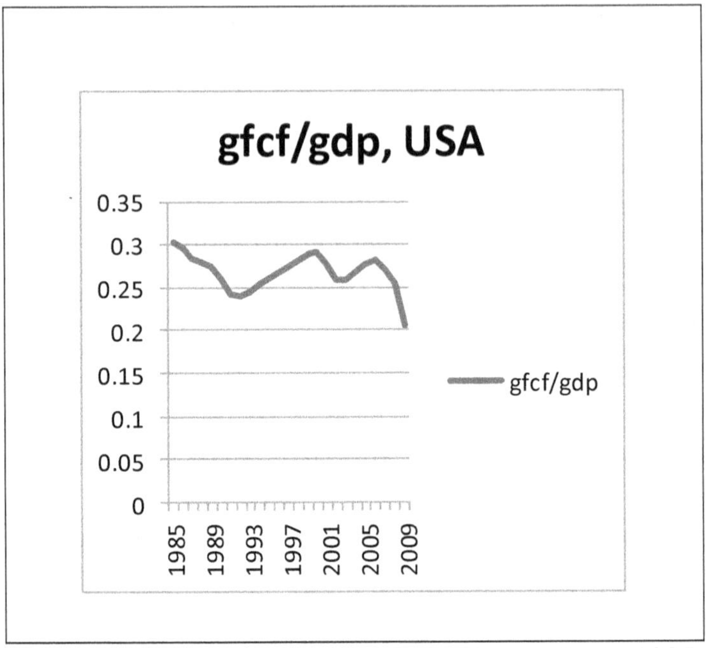

Figure 18, Gross fixed capital formation to GNP, 1985-2009.

The shocks of 1990s, and 2001, are much smaller than the new one at 2007-2008. That requires substantial reallocation of resources to domestic capital formation activities.[28] That does not mean tax break for the 1 percent, hedge fund managers, billionaires. The fixed, physical capital, which produces income revenues, and jobs for the middle class workers is the kind of capital is strongly recommend. That is physical and human capital, housing, professors, and teaching, jobs, electronics, technology jobs, which actually employ people in production, which increases the tax revenues, not just more tollbooths, fee collectors, and robotics.

Figure 18, and Figure 4, Growth and decay rates of after tax income for United States, 2004-2009, are disquieting data in my estimations, we need not add social and cultural war fuels to them. Unfortunately, in time of economic decay these Jim Crow practices become mortal self-inflecting economic wounds, and they become more common. We have known states in Deep South that have never pulled themselves up by their victimized minorities bootstraps, until, they became Toyota republicans, and after the civil laws were passed. It is sad to see their retro-regressive proclivities, and their economically consequential slide backs.

Some great companies have come in along, great American auto industries. You noted some of the other industries were mentioned. A proposed study by author looks at modular production (in books Teconomics, Teconometrics) approach could apply to digital and internet multimedia, and filmic production industries can reduce cascading downturns. I have also argued in this research that housing and related industries, because they are regional, and they have immobile nature, they can have economic growth and development influences, historically.

It has been consequential that garnishing hostile transactional intentions, legalistic exclusionary and odd localisms practices, the southern strategies prejudices, in courtrooms, boardrooms, and classrooms will have great many sustained negative economic externalities. Their co-existence with the new decentralized multimedia age spotlights introduces transpicuous presences, which determines their existential terminable inevitability.[29]

The ratios of gross capital formation to nominal gross national product decay rates in its repetitions has more to convey to us, than its economic origin. Investments are more than a simple economic decision. When you purchase a house, you check out the neighborhood, schools, shops, medical centers, social and religious hubs, chain stores, and local government. The buyers, investors study and internalize risks and uncertainties for the next thirty years of those mortgages.

Utah has been bobbing around the low water marks for sometimes. It is time for the citizenry in Utah to take a national leadership role to realize the negative fruits of that misguided labor, and put legislative term-limits, criminal background checks, and removal by petitions for all political offices. It is good for two parties' presidential office, too. It will be even greater for state political offices and the states' economies. A history of xenophobic, homophobic, sexists', racists' lawlessness, and retaliatory hate and vengeance laws cannot produce good laws for the states or nations. No legal-good will come out of Dr. Mangle's nation-state laboratories. Forget the presidency for a longer while, until we educate you more of global fragilities and sustainability, before you move in. Learn something from your mistaken laws faster.

When people of a book, whom had experienced the Missouri fiasco of 1883, formulate or engage in historical errors and inhumanity of Mountain Meadow Massacre, you hope they have reached cultural maturity to refrain from anti-constitutional laws against others. Utah has demonstrated that intellectual maturity many times. It is very disappointing, when the people or nations let themselves done by following the least intellects among them over the edge of histrionics. I knew at least two presidents of church, which would have counseled vigorously against such miss-conducts under the glare of history, and of Allah, and God. There are no reasons to deny great Mormons their participations in the functional democracy, if they are not denying others rights to the same constitutional democracy.

It is a known fact that well over 80 percent of Utah politicians are white male Mormons, that legislations are filtered and controlled by church overtly. Important federal laws have gone unenforced for centuries. One example is a viral criminal polygamy with child-rape and chronic child molestations. Even officers of the courts, attorney general, police leaders are not immune from the fanatical vicious attacks, name-calling, and political intrigues against them, when they fight such bad practices. They are also members of LDS church. Unfortunately, in that kind of atmosphere with Republican Party legacies of the last administration and their phobic-fearful-isms a culture of victimization bears more rotten fruits.

However, self-filtering unconstitutional laws often works in most states, accept in these times of national digressions, the one party church control conservatism can implode in anti-immigration state-laws. At no times, it is a bright idea to start from illegal (unconstitutional) premises, and proceed to bad laws. Then try to sell it as a good or legal notion or laws. That was and is foolhardy.

The torture gang, which had the full support of Utah representatives, is presently coconspirators in breaking the law. They are often convicted in the court of public opinions, without even seeing a judge. They will serve a life sentence as Nixon did. Those who have initiated a series of unconstitutional state laws from the premise of anti-civil laws, anti-constitutional laws, and of racial and national profiling will meet even a harsher penalty than public condemnations, no matter how they fool themselves and their cadres and dominions into lawlessness. They can find themselves out of political office, too.

The notions of something bad, evil, catastrophic happened, therefore, we can break all these laws, discard the constitution, these conventions, those legal practices, such ethical norms, and our moral premises are foolish in law, as they are foolish in commonsense. It is imbecilic in practice, and it will offend all senses. It will often backfire with disastrous results. Those promised and fleeting glimpses of dignity and hope will become falling stars faster than you can say Abu Gharib, permanent wars, war pictures, suspect thrashings, lost prospective, lost lives, and lost international arguments, and leadership positions.

It is important for Utah citizenry to recognize all aspects of the economic decays, which follows the culture of victimizations they have recently uncharacteristically embraced.[30] They will bury, lie, and distort the impacts of such laws, but it will come. The infamy of torture-fiasco did not mushroom into global shame, with its huge costs initially, or because we did not try to hide it. We already heard reports that some legislators threaten retaliation against law enforcement, which will not enforce bill of tenders and anti-constitutional laws. Even media (fake media) has been attacked for opining about it, or carrying out their 4th pillar-duties of first amendment. Once again, proof positives, such xenophobic, profiling, and discriminatory laws have been institutionalized in education, in jobs, in government employments, they need to be monitored and cleansed.

They systematically keep the minorities out of educational opportunities, out of the job market, and then they blame them for failing and under performances of their failing economies. They attack the ACLU. They attack college educators, now they attack legal profession and low enforcements.

These require national analysis and scrutiny. We have established laws against these nonsenses. We have brushed our national shames under the rug with a few dollar bribes and forced apologies, but they go right back at it, making the same mistakes. We need not look back to McCarthyism epoch.[31] We have had the 40 odd years of harmed lives and history of slavery to see the illegal harm of xenophobic bigoted handiworks and run away negative externalities, and social costs of slavery, neo-peonage, and sexism, and the xenophobic abstractionisms.

The economic impact of such unconstitutional acts will appear with small and gradual drying of capital out of the Jim Crow cities and states. First tax increase on property and income and higher fees will be a direct attempt to replace the capital flight, but soon the jobs and income limitations will dry that up, beside human capital flight is often faster and more devastating. There are often more tainted reasons for the chronic decays.[32] However, the characters, nature, and rate of decay changes the longer the deteriorations continue.

Local authorities often gear up enforcement to fight general blight and increased crimes. However, as chronic blight sets, attracting, or bribing capital will become more complicated, and costlier. The cities and states fall in sustained chronic blight. Skilled educated workers and investors (wise-capital, smart money) do not venture in chronic blight states, they often leave them as soon as possible, sometime with losses, unless government intervene (Federal and State investments or guarantees). Good educators, law enforcers, professionals also are chased or hired away. States will decide how to modify and reduce friction, increase inducements, seek and encourage Federal interventions and investments, or join the blight.

State of Bless, or Chronic State of Blight

Behind door, number one there may be the state of bless, behind door number two there may be the state of blight. Nevertheless, how and why would a functional economy find the wrong door?

Next figure shows the bucket experiments, for two economies. One economy propagates economic growth, appropriate investments in education, job retraining, balance redistribution by jobs, and dynamic circular flow models. Two, this economy is into wealth concentration, phantom supply side remedies, and gimmicky statistical manipulations, and restrictive capital and labor mobility. Both economies start with a hypothetical $17 trillion, the former redistributes all of it by jobs, bottom up higher velocity of money. The latter, redistributes most of its capital funds to about 10, 5, or 1 percent of population in hope they will create jobs.

All three buckets start full, they will contain 10, 7, 3 (20 gallons) of water. The +17 side, in the three-buckets economy (instead of 20 gallons, we have 17 gallons) it notes that in macroeconomics 85 percent of capacity is considered full capacity. Assume the 3 gallons are spillage in the water example, bad ideas, waste, and fraud, etc.

The next water experiment starts with all three buckets full with 20 gallons of water. Then we place the 3 gallons bucket in the 7 gallons bucket, and both of them in the 10 gallons bucket. Now there is 10 gallons spillage, and only 10 gallons of water is left more or less, in the one-bucket economy.[33] Wrong austerity plans, structural unemployment, joblessness, military consumptive growth, underinvestment in R&D, and education, upward misdistributions of wealth (and income) will use up the $ 7 trillion fast.

That is why the art and sciences of getting out of bad recessions are left to the real professionals, the economists. You will vote on this bucket experiments, you will pick one, in this next election. The former three bucket economy, there are jobs, and tax revenues to pay for infrastructures, proper balance in the economy. In the latter, there are fewer jobs, miserliness, and parsimony prevails. Fears of joblessness, curtails consumptive demands, and fear of economic conditions abstains futuristic job creation by supply-side innovation and expansion. Predatory hedge-fund expansions or investments, which can act like microeconomic creative destructions, do not sustain the aggregate economic conditions. Figure 19 shows the buckets experiments.[34] It shows the importance of balance budgeting in economies.

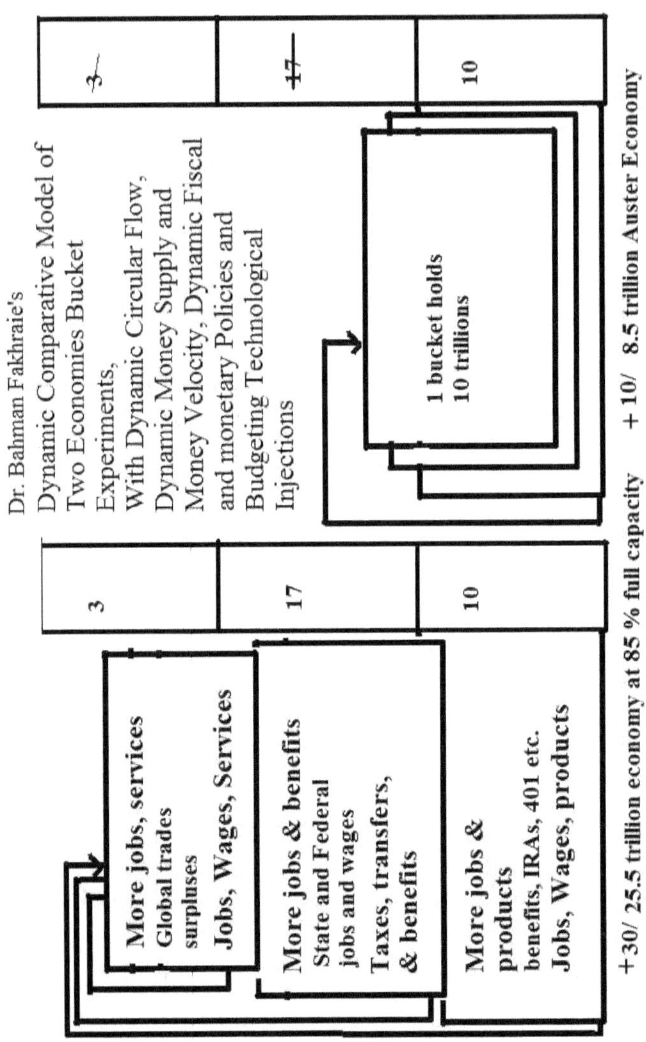

Figure 19, Dynamic comparative bucket experiments model of austerity in two economies.

Behind door number three, there may be disaster, or rupture, take your picks. Next time you visit certain over sea and a few African state-nations try to study which ones have fallen in chronic state of blights and will never get out, under the same bad governance. Let us learn something before we all fall in such state of economic blight. However, it is often easy to point at the hinterland and opine philosophically corrective remedies at others expense. In healing thyself, everyone will need educated, entrepreneurial, even international, constructionists, friends.

In the following figure, the economy is growing with technological injection in a balanced, sustainable way to accommodate natural rate of growth of the population and mild inflationary pressure associated with growth of middle class jobs, new graduates' salaries.[35] The profits are not going in the pockets of the executives, hedge fund managers, (seriously, like the last 3 decades). In addition, at E2, the technology monopoly profits, as some new technology business generate. It does not go in the pockets of a soul owner, making fast track billionaires. It is properly taxed and redistributed, one in appropriate salaries to workers, and union workers. Two, it goes to sustain the society that generates the tolerable atmosphere to encourage the entrepreneurial culture and activities. The soul creators are not plagiarized out of their important contributions, recognitions, their incomes, profits, and millions. However, the society is not cheated out of their sustainable, tax and transfer, appropriate dynamic circular flow.[36] Therefore, at E3, qt3 is purchased with more jobs, and lower prices than at E2. Figure 20 shows Technology injections, growth, jobs, and prices.

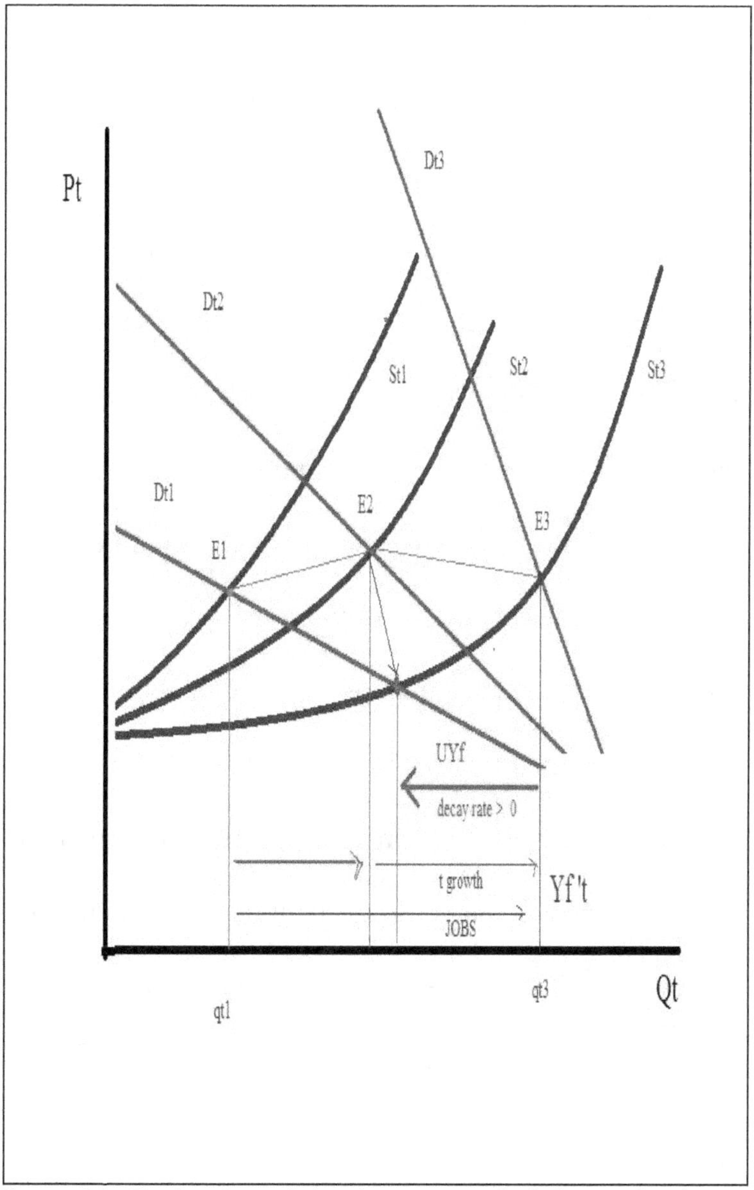

Figure 20, Technology injections, growth, jobs, and prices.

Not all is lost yet, especially in a country that is big and big hearted by its people. Therefore, when well-meaning political leaders find a quicksilver bullet solution, which will make thousands unemployed, and keep real disposable income low for three decades, they want to cheat the earned benefits of elderlies, and they want to undermined the heath care of their population, you know they have missed the mark. Especially, if they want to make new graduates, teachers, postal and government workers unemployed, you know, they are really off the mark, and off their rockers, intellectually speaking. Technology-growth shows increase in prices and quantities and jobs.[37] Thus a macro fiscal and monetary policies, (or the Federal Reserve Bank policies), which encourage growth with a mild (controlled) inflationary pressures are essentials.

Here is a graph to perk you right up. It is the growth rate of real gross national product per population of United States for years 2001to 2008. However, there is no time for complacency. It is important to realize that distortions in redistribution are often hidden, and different indices can only reveal portion of the truth. Nevertheless, the growth rate of income per capital shows promises. However, it will still be in the job creation that the true magic of real economic powerhouse of free competitive but well-functioning democracy can perform especially well.

Figure 28 shows the real per capital grow and fell after 2007.[38] It generally fell to 44-45 thousand dollars levels. Therefore, a decent stimulus injection and infrastructure reconstruction would pay more dividends by now. It could have improved the job numbers. It would have increased the tax revenues. Moreover, it would have helped the reelection of existing government. None of the silly wars can ever do that much. Political rhetoric heat up in recessions of business cycles. The less economically informed agents could engage in hyperbole beyond the maximum capacity of the fully employed economy. However, in early post-recession period, that kind hyperbole can inject more unhealthy uncertainty and fear, and shake up the trust issues enough to discourage growth-pushes needed out of the recessions. Grant you, those specific investments and multipliers are required. That cannot be confused as the death of mixed economies.[39] This area requires much more research, and fine-tuning, before the last calls, so do not discard the macroeconomic instruments (and fiscal-tools), even with dysfunctional politics.[40] A fiscal new branch of a central bank can jar the political parties, or awaken the Zombies enough to help. Figure 21 shows the real per capital grow and fell after 2007.

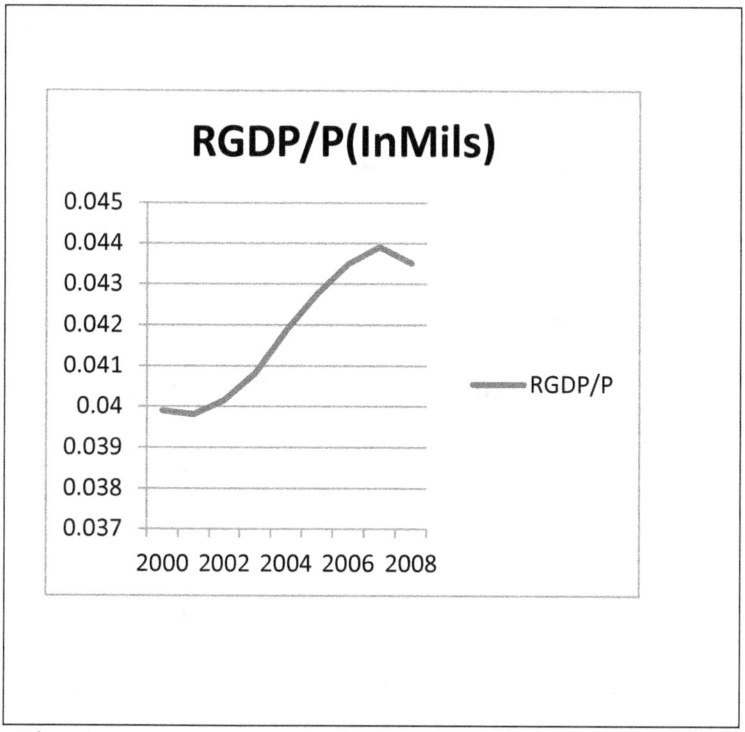

Figure 21, USA growth and decay rates of real GDP per capita, 2000-2008 USA.

Therefore, unemployment is particularly pernicious, at the tail end of multiple economic down turns. In figure 28, this is shown by lower prices and less employment and rate of decay.

We have to realize that technological injections can performs very well, if the well-functioning free competitive economy establishes adoptive tools to remedy severe alienation of certain obsolete jobs, by retraining, and available remedies, other than political demagogy. A few months of unemployment in modern time, is the difference between middle class and poor status. When structural unemployment are added to the mix, income (wage)-tax-transfer are out of balance, the economy will not sustain any long-term growth. In addition, the political consequences develop with very abrupt characteristic, as well. So, bump the deficit higher, again, with moderate inflated dollars, so it will be more, and still do the same things, and spend it on real job making investments and infrastructure. You will adjust the wages and incomes, to induce higher aggregate demands at E3 (in figure 24). You can look at the same half full and half-empty glass and say it is half-full or half-empty, however, you cannot get more than half of a glass out of it, until you fill it up, all the way. in case of 1929-1940 president Roosevelt (FDR) found it all empty, and he had to refill it all the way up by policy, we do not need to do that much yet, if we get over the dysfunctional do-nothing part.

At least for now, in true (real) democracies, voting or petitioning out bad legislators and agents of intolerance, and removing their handiworks are still probable. Utah citizenry like New Yorkers will join California political theoretically bifurcated party systems, their population, and their governors, in reintroducing corrective balance back in their political lives.[41] After all, they have lived in sunshine under their dominant theology for a long time. They ought to know better. Intolerance does not advance their causes, their people principles and their good deeds do, their inclusivity unifies their forces and increases velocity of money and repairs aggregate demand shortfalls. They need to invest, and hire for good jobs, so the actual turnarounds in the economy occur. That is true for all states, from Oregon, and Washington, to Florida and Texas.

Economies do make comebacks. After a few decades of close observation of internal working of theoretical and applied economic policies, it is important to study how assumptive foundations by one team are totally ignored and abundant by another team, without the foresights of the eventualities.

Economies do make comebacks and get through bad times, however, it is important that both parties understand they are working on the same construction of the same national building, and everyone else had to be in on the good time, since they have all been in for the bad times. Income distributions, livable- jobs matter, they matter to sustain a functional economy, and cohesive government. Thriving economies are not zero sum games, global trade and resources sharing through the market mechanisms are not zero sum games. That is where militarism misleads and self-harms economies, and starves them. The more constructively positive, and sustainable economic models require functioning domestic none military components, where free markets and governments play constructively positive and predominant rules in sustainability and functionality of those economic models.

Summery

The reason for such economic disasters are more complex than the complex financial tools, people used, when they did not understand them. There are still financial forces and actors there willing to ignore some or all of the forces that complies the economic disasters of this millennium. It is important to enumerate a few important ones, so we notice the good changes when the resurrections ascend among us.

1. Conversions of negative externalities on technological steroids, associated with many bad decisions become catastrophically pronounced.
2. Real disposable income declines over past three decades.
3. Age composition of workers and taxpayers influences tax-transfer ratios. Combined with deportation policy, lead to government revenue shortages due to replacement shortages of high-income earners, financial supporters, and employers.
4. Hostile comprehensive anti-immigration policies domestically increased the potency of industrial competitors globally.

5. Resending depression epochs' firewall-laws in favor of too-big-to-fail profiteering arrangements added to the mischiefs.
6. Monopoly, oligopoly, oligarchic market power shifts influencing union-management, redistribution-mechanisms, power-structures, profits, wages (ratios of CEO pays to workers' pay averages), taxes (billionaires' rates vs. Middle-Class taxes), earned benefits and fees settings, in many key industries (investment banking, War industries, multinational media, Energy, Mega internet technology sectors and industries, etc.)
7. The infiltrated, corrupted, motivated military-security-political-industrial-complex could not let a profitable self-leaking ice cream of BenLadenism-terrorism, Alt-right extremisms parish, without litigious-excesses, and domestic litigious

overreach, and massive unproductive investments in fixed obsolete war machines and concrete buildings.

8. War deficit funding, without required tax increases added to war economic psychosis and fear-security spending without required balancing tax increases (and tax breaks of the highest' income earners).
9. Use of complex financial instruments, without studies by private research or academic analysis, yielded bad finance modeling and its consequences.
10. False risk-loan ratios induced hyper-economic activities cause bobble formations and busts.
11. Domestic anchor-industry destructions (housing) based on incomprehensible financial tools, based on false risk-mortgage ratios.
12. Later, post 9-11 fear-security issues led to destructions of secondary industries (travel and

hospitality industries, agriculture) by reactionary and accumulative legalisms, immigration extreme laws, and TSA-type excesses, all of anti-civil law and anti-constitution acts, and harmful anti-privacy intrusive laws.

13. Conversions of multiple-negative economic forces, at the time of dysfunctional politicizations and representative inactions to counter balance them.
14. A classic demand-depression declines and cascading consequence met austerity mantras.
15. Subversion of the supply side tax break remedies, into tax avoidance and wealth concentration strategies.
16. Harmful influences on capital formation, on small business job creation, on educational, on research and development funding, by diminutions.

17. Sevier under funding of infrastructure projects for political motives.
18. They should raise the one presenters' taxes 5 percent, and establish an alternative cooperate minimum tax for the tax avoidance INCs, to help pay for the other two wars, they started. They forget they did this from social security lockbox, but they swiftly transferred the revenue into tax breaks for the highest incomes.
19. SCHADENFREUDES, dysfunctional governance to undercut a minority run administration facing complex problems patterns.
20. Americans ought not to worry about the elderlies' Social Security, Earned Benefits and Medicare, their school ages' schools and teachers, workers, their gardeners, and nurses, their hospitality staffs, hotel and motel house-cleaners. Their Hollywood

stars and visiting guests, their firefighters, and their police officers, postal persons and professors, their incarcerated youth and immigrant relatives, their vanishing educated scholars, and the jobs they can create, they are all on the menu, with the rest of middle class America.

When people euphorically try to over sell you on the new growth explosion and economic utopia, remind yourselves, how many of these factors have expanded, remedied, or diminished, before joining the euphoric madness of the mobs. When these many variables go wrong and no one has a clue, or not all clues are discovered, by regulators, by market expert, by markets, by media, you know you will see it again in your lifetime. Nevertheless, the power is in your votes. Most importantly, the logic is in your heads. Use them both, to sustain your futures. No one else has that power.

In a democracy, and not an oligarchy or plutocracy, it is your vote, transparency, knowledge, and accountability, and term-limits for a backstop, if anything goes wrong, which often does, your vote is wasted too. A big crowd behind the wrong person or persons is a dangerous capital-destructive mob. All excuses can be used to influence your knowledge, transparency, and their term limits. Therefore, people have to keep on top of events, information, and their votes.

Ignoring economic issues of these magnitudes, because technological injections magnify their forces, it will not make them disappear. It will make the problems larger, more hurtful, and more expensive to cure. Perhaps, that cap of chai with the diplomats will be better for all sides, than the dark espresso with war conciliar, in the chai-khaneh of modernity.

Economies, macroeconomics can help countries recover, if the national will and the resolves are there to encourage the elected representatives into the needed positive actions. And, when the corrected assumptive-market models are chosen constructively, cooperatively, compassionately, positively, and wisely economies will progress positively.

Great countries have surprised humanity with their positive national resolves, when they have engendered the inclusive and all-encompassing forces of creative constructivism. Nevertheless, it is true. You can only eat an elephant, one bite at a time. Moreover, a long journey starts with the first decided step. Perhaps, an optimistic outlook, inclusive world vision, and cooperative and compassionate spirits are more than a theological need, but part of discovering futuristic outlook for life long travelers, to improve human conditions. Long past sentimentality, a cautious view of mild humanities' economic growth does not abolish the human historical progressions on sustainable economic roads. We have done it in the past. We will do it again, now or in our near future.

Notes

[1] James Diamond, Warren Buffet, Donald Trump, Murdock, and the Gates among others have expressed their positive attitudes about the American experiences. We all have an interest to see the ship of state stays afloat.

[2] Warren E. Buffett, *Stop Coddling the Super-Rich*, New York Times 8-14-2011 http://www.nytimes.com/2011/08/15/opinion/stop-coddling-the-super-rich.html

[3] Mr. Buffett stated, "But what I paid was only 17.4 of my taxable income — and that's actually a lower percentage than was paid by any of the other 20 people in our office. Their tax burdens ranged from 33 percent to 41 percent and averaged 36 percent.
Last year about 80 percent of these revenues came from personal income taxes and payroll taxes. The mega-rich pay income taxes at a rate of 15 percent on most of their earnings but pay practically nothing in payroll taxes. It's a different story for the middle class: typically, they fall into the 15 percent and 25 percent income tax brackets, and then are hit with heavy payroll taxes to boot." Ibid.

[4] "Since 1992, the I.R.S. has compiled data from the returns of the 400 Americans reporting the largest income. In 1992, the top 400 had aggregate taxable income of $16.9 billion and paid federal taxes of 29.2 percent on that sum. In 2008, the aggregate income of the highest 400 had

soared to $90.9 billion — a staggering $227.4 million on average — but the rate paid had fallen to 21.5 percent." ibid.

[5] Alas, here Mr. Buffet says, " I would leave rates for 99.7 percent of taxpayers unchanged and continue the current 2-percentage-point reduction in the employee contribution to the payroll tax. This cut helps the poor and the middle class, who need every break they can get.
But for those making more than $1 million — there were 236,883 such households in 2009 — I would raise rates immediately on taxable income in excess of $1 million, including, of course, dividends and capital gains. And for those who make $10 million or more — there were 8,274 in 2009 — I would suggest an additional increase in rate." Ibid

[6] Three republican senators stood in the USA senate retanda to confront the bent against American healthcare. They may have saved an obselet institution of republicanism. By CARL HULSE, McCain Provides a Dramatic Finale on Health Care: Thumb Down, JULY 28, 201, https://www.nytimes.com/2017/07/28/us/john-mccains-real-return.html
Gail Collins, Susan Collins and Lisa Murkowski, the Health Vote Heroines, JULY 28, 2017 https://www.nytimes.com/2017/07/28/opinion/health-susan-collins-murkowski.html?action=click&contentCollection=U.S.&module=Trending&version=Full&region=Marginalia&pgtype=article

[7] "America is at a fragile and critical moment in its history. We must restore hope in the American Dream. We must celebrate all that America stands for around the world. And while our Founding Fathers[7] recognized the constructive value of political debate, we must send the message to today's elected officials in a civil, respectful voice they hear and understand that the time to put citizenship ahead of partisanship is now." Howard Schultz, *Starbucks CEO urges boycott of campaign money, by* Catalina Camia, USA TODAY Updated 2011-08-16 7:35 PM http://content.usatoday.com/communities/onpolitics/post/2011/08/starbucks-campaign-donations-howard-schultz-/1

[8] …"First, to withhold political campaign contributions until a transparent, comprehensive, bipartisan debt-and-deficit package is reached that honestly, and fairly, sets America on a path to long-term financial health and security. Second, to do all we can to break the cycle of economic uncertainty that grips our country by committing to accelerate investment in jobs and hiring"
Howard Schultz, *Starbucks CEO urges boycott of campaign money, by* Catalina Camia, USA TODAY Updated 2011-08-16 7:35 PM
http://content.usatoday.com/communities/onpolitics/post/2011/08/starbucks-campaign-donations-howard-schultz-/1
Joe Norcera, Boycott Campaign Donations! August 12, 2011
http://www.nytimes.com/2011/08/13/opinion/nocera-boycott-campaign-donations.html?_r=1&pagewanted=print

[9] Note. Calculation and graph by author.

Gross Collections, by Type of Tax, Fiscal Years 1960–2010 http://www.irs.gov/taxstats/article/0,,id=171960,00.html

[10] organized into ERS/USDA Baseline countries and regions historical population and growth rates in population for Baseline countries/regions 1969-2010. Updated: July 20, 2010 based on June 2010 Census Bureau update.

[11] Binyamin Appelbaum, Inside the Fed in 2006: A Coming Crisis, and Banter, New York Times, 1,12,2012, http://www.nytimes.com/2012/01/13/business/transcripts-show-an-unfazed-fed-in-2006.html?_r=2&partner=rss&emc=rss&pagewanted=print

[12] Backup Data: CBO's Year-by-Year Forecast and Projections for Calendar Years 2011 to 2021, (and Actual Data for Calendar Years 1950 to 2010). Published in, *The Budget and Economic Outlook: An Update August* 2011).

[13] Note: author calculation from, source,http://data.bls.gov/timeseries/CES0000000001?output_view=net_1mth

[14] Econometricians are economists who study economic data statistically. Teconometricians, are define by author in Teconomic book, they are economists that do iteration and statistically study technological injection in modern economy.

[15] http://thecritical-post.com/blog/2011/12/president-obamas-speech-about-economy-at-osawatomie-high-school-in-osawatomie-kansas-6-december-2011-transcript-text-tcpchicago/

[16] 1) Refers to individuals aged 15 to 24 in private households,
excluding those in military service or civilian alternative
2) Trend estimate for Germany, Finland, Austria
3) For the reporting month of April 2011
4) For the reporting month of March 2011
5) Youth unemployment in Europe1) (seasonally adjusted2) results from workforce surveys in June 2011)
6) http://www.spiegel.de/international/europe/0,1518,779906,00.html

[17] One of Senator Teddy Kennedy's favorite idioms read more in his book also a good antidote in Senator Arlen Spector's recent book.

[18] There have been a large number of cases that ended in financial fines, without admission of criminal intend; however, the problems persist, thus the reason for claw back laws. Louise Story and Gretchen Morgenson, "S.E.C. Accuses Goldman of Fraud in Housing Deal," *New York Times*, April 16, 2010,

http://www.nytimes.com/2010/04/17/business/17goldman.html?_r=2&pagewanted=print

[19] " Credit default swaps are financial instruments that serve to protect against a default by a particular bond or security.

They were invented by Wall Street in the late 1990s as a form of insurance. Between 2000 and 2008, the market for such swaps ballooned from $900 billion to more than $30 trillion. In sharp contrast to traditional insurance, swaps are totally unregulated. They played a pivotal role in the global financial meltdown in late 2008"
Credit Default Swaps, New York Times, Updated: March 9, 2012
http://topics.nytimes.com/top/reference/timestopics/subjects/c/credit_default_swaps/index.html?inline=nyt-classifier

[20] Commonly these formulations hold, (Qc> Qo> Qm, and Pm>Po>Pc) read Fellner (1949) for more on implications of "fewness",
William J. Fellner, *Competition Among the Few*, New York, Augustus m. Kelley Publisher, 1965, 10-11

[21] Unlike the recent GSA misspending, or unwise militarisms, research and development and education generates 3 to 1 returns, auditing and governmental general auditors propagate 12 to 1 returns on investment. C. Subramanian, " GSA Scandal: So What Does $823,000 Buy You in Las Vegas?" *Time* 4, 18, 2012,
http://newsfeed.time.com/2012/04/18/gsa-scandal-so-what-does-823000-buy-you-in-las-vegas/
D. Nakamura and E. O'Keefe, "*Inquiry points to wider Secret Service scandal involving as many as 21 women,*" *USA TODAY*, 4, 17, 2012,
http://www.usatoday.com/news/washington/story/2012-04-17/secret-service-scandal/54349978/1

[22] 4 years BS, MS PhD, prof, This is excluding associate degree (commercial inst.)

Integrated post-secondary education data(IPED)
US Metro Areas ranked by Per Capita Income, 2006. Released April 24, 2008,
http://www.skyscrapercity.com/showthread.php?t=614249
Dr. Bahman Fakhraie research and regression analysis, on limited sample data.
Federal reserve Bank of New York, current issues, income and finance, v17,no6, www.newyorkfed.org/research/current_issues

[23] Table 1.1.4. Price Indexes for Gross Domestic Product (Index numbers, 2000=100)
Annual data from 1929 To 2007
Bureau of Economic Analysis
Data published October 30, 2008
File created 10/29/2008 8:58:12 AM
Author calculated the income cross elasticity of three variables

[24] When inexperienced macroeconomists apply Keynes, they think, every purchase is an investment. However, the multiplier-effect is more pronounced, with the investments in income earning assets (capital) with different rates of returns, amount, quality, and duration of productivity matters.

[25] There is more than transient evidence that capital formation iterated, econometrically defined and measures as in recent dissertation, influences the overall economy.

[26] GDP by type for expenditures and value added by kind of economic activity, annual, from 1970-2009. UNCATAD, UNTADstat, United Nation, Data.

[27] UN, data for Algeria, Australia, Iran, US, UK, etc., for all of the nations were used and they all showed the same, exact inflections using the ratios, GFCF, or GCF/GDP. That is why author recommends the iterations and econometrics to get around the duplicative and potential-template errors.

[28] Dr. Bahman Fakhraie Dissertation

[29] Its technological-negative impact on aspect of militarism was demonstrated earlier. It is beyond wide-eyed suppositions, in the thick scientific theory now. It garnished financial costs, damages.

[30] Utah and Mormons in particular will get a lot of press. They have confronted anti-social offshoots in polygamy cults. Let me suggest a few books. Most importantly is "Remembering Uncle Golden" about J. Golden Kimball. It will dissuade harsh judgments on all Morons. They do not all deserve it.

[31] By JAMES RISEN and TOM RISENJUNE, Donald Trump Does His Best Joe McCarthy Impression , 22, 2017 https://www.nytimes.com/2017/06/22/opinion/sunday/donald-trump-joseph-mccarthy-west-virginia.html

[32] New PRRI/The Atlantic Survey Analysis Finds Cultural Displacement—Not Economic Hardship—More Predictive of White Working-Class Support for Trump, 05.09.2017 https://www.prri.org/press-release/white-working-class-attitudes-economy-trade-immigration-election-donald-trump/

[33] That is less by the masses of the two added buckets, so less than 10 gallons, precisely.

[34] Read more on different circular-flow technological injections https://order.proquest.com/OA_HTML/pqdtibeCCtpItmDspRte.jsp

[35] Author has presented elements of sustainability lemma in at least an earlier paper, and three more recent books.

[36] Dr. Bahman Fakhraie in "Teconomics, Microeconomics" introduced the econometrics and arithmetic of sustainability lemma, and "Supply and Demand of technological Injection," and "Technological Injection... " books. It involves more equations, than real interest rates.

[37] Late professor Milton Freedman favored 3 percent money growth, to encourage 3 or higher GDP growth, I favored up to 6.5 percent assumptive increases, to insure 3-6 present dig-out-of-recession real growth, and later the 3 percent real growth for sustainability, with slightly positive real rate of interests. That is (i-B □ 0). 1970s and 1980s, proved the need for more stimulus like the present economy. Thus, the Dr. Paul Walker solution, at about 18 percent interest for inflation slayers, was the backstop for the runaway inflation. Except, that income misdistribution is more pronounced now. Professors Lance Girton and Don Roper did more research on the mathematical aspect of real interest rates.

[38] Source: calculation, and graph presentation were by author.

CBO, published in *The Budget and Economic Outlook: An Update August* 2011.

[39] Now, academics rule out assumptive portions of some theories, reject hypothetical and propositional misstatement severely. But, they do not < violently > bury theories. Well, because Zombies do come back and bite! Besides, there are a lot of research, wisdom, and money supplies behind the statements in the following research. (Dr. Bernanke's national classes, 2012)
James Bullard, "Death of a Theory," Federal Reserve Bank of St. Louise *Review*, March/April 2012, 94(2), 83-101

[40] James Bullard, "Death of a Theory," Federal Reserve Bank of St. Louise *Review*, March/April 2012, 94(2), 83-101

[41] <bahf_econ © 4/11/2009 UOU, UT USA>, the dates show, some parts of this book were written and copyrighted earlier by author, some predate the economic crash of 2008, some go backs decades earlier, and they are adopted for this publications. All rights are reserved by Dr. Bahman Fakhraie

(From front matter)

Let stay human in your heart,

And let the nescience heads flee

Then even a mystic can divine you,

The mysteries of love

Let knowledge find you,

And let ignorance flee

Then, a mystic will divine you

The mysteries of your lives

§§§§ dr.bahf.econ © 2011 9-20-11

THE END

APPENDIX

A

The Lagrange Formulation, Sheppard Lemmas

$$Q = f\,(vi) \text{ for } vi > 0$$

And

$$L = f\,(vi)-(y-(c.vi)) = 0$$

Minimization condition,

First order condition,

$$\frac{\partial L}{\partial t} = 0$$

Second order condition,

$$\frac{\partial L^2}{\partial t} \geq 0$$

Maximization condition,

First order condition,

$$\frac{\partial L}{\partial t} = 0$$

Second order condition,

$$\frac{\partial L^2}{\partial t} \leq 0$$

fvi fvn > (fvi vn) ^{2}

Thus, $\forall$, Vi > 0 (i= 1. 2. 3….n)

APPENDIX

B

Sustainability Lemmas, Rules, and Conditions

Author's books, " Teconomic," and "Technological injection..." contain analysis that is more extensive. Some of author's older (copyrighted works) were also helpful.

$$\forall \ Vi > 0 \quad (i= 1.\ 2.\ 3\ldots.n)$$

$$\frac{\partial Pt}{\partial AVCt} \geq 0$$

Ceteris Paribus (caeteris paribus)

$$\frac{\partial Wt}{\partial t} \geq \text{0-3 percent}$$

Ceteris Paribus

$$\frac{\partial RDI_t}{\partial t} \geq \text{0-3 percent}$$

Mutatis Mutandis

$$\frac{\partial MS}{\partial t} \geq 3 - 6 \text{ percent}$$

Ceteris Paribus

$$\frac{\partial \pi}{\partial t} \geq 0 - 3 \text{ percent}, \text{ given } (r - i = B)^*$$

Mutatis Mutandis

$$\frac{\partial RDI_2}{\partial t} \geq \text{0-3 percent}$$

Mutatis Mutandis

$$\frac{\partial gdp_d}{\partial t} \geq (3-6)\text{percent}$$

Mutatis Mutandis

APPENDIX

C

Comprehensive Immigration, Naturalization, USA Job Creation Dream Act of 2013

The Comprehensive Immigration, Naturalization, USA Job Creation Dream Act of 2013 can pass. Or it can pass during the administration of President B. H. Obama's second term.

Family Unification, (speeding up areas)

a) Immediate family units' unifications, **Residency card fast trucks 15 year main option**, with automatic citizenship track reserves with limited proposal causes to delay, on filing paper works, or intend. Establish a **onetime fee** for all of the processes, [hbt+r+c > c+r > r] as options and choices, with the same A number for the onetime payment and proof of payment (cccard receipt, check or stab, tickets etc.) Denying or delaying citizenship is removed without substantiated probable cause, and if 60 precent of requirement are met. (Include criminal activities, as cause for naturalization process delay, but not detention or deportation, if not proven, or on hearsay, unless criminal gang or serious harm is intended, terrorism, etc.). After 5 year- residency, a 3-year quick citizenship on probation for good conducts no criminal records, if they speak English, know history and math, (or passes citizenship in that time).

b) Shut operational double-dipping mushrooming, cost explosion, fake job duplication instead of job creation, and mission creep expansive budget chumming. Privacy violations, total information traps, expenses build ups, and overcharging, community spying instead of policing, and turf expansions without probable causes, local service intrusions or take over without budget controls.
c) Relation visits, education, tourist's temporaries.

PhDs, Masters, (BS, MBAs, investment residencies, business persons, entrepreneurial team members, speed up areas (possible republican representative sing along section), and students whom acquire one post graduate degrees in United States. These types of individuals with children grown, educated in USA for more than 20,20,30, years should receive category one priorities, military volunteers, registered, military spouse, category two. Please, give the judges freedom to speed up, and clear with good judgment-calls expeditiously, and grant citizenship, when productive track record, educational history, job-creation intends indicates it. This has been an important legacy aspect of American historical success, American exceptionalness, and American generosity, and American democracy, free market, and entrepreneurial spirit, which should endure small mindedness, and competitive industrial complexes to purchase the political inroads to defeat this dynamic American experimentation in job creation, and job growth.

d) Residency 5 year max, the 3 year quick citizenship on probation for good conducts no criminal records, if speech English, knows history and math, (or passes citizenship in that time). Naturalization, after 5 to 8 years.

Legal quack mires, snafus, bottle-necks, screw ups. **Clean up areas**

e) Clean up areas; stay until the legal situations are cleared. Children with one degree, extend residency with 15 year options to automatic citizenship tracks, allow them to nominate parents, unless the join the services military or any federal, state, local, tribal governmental-service entities. Then put on the 3-years quick citizenship on probation for good conducts no criminal records, if speak English, knows history and math, (or passes citizenship in that time).

f) Unless developing criminal records, become criminal or drug gangs' members, etc.

* Illegals, workers (hb1, agro workers, temporary seasonal, with tax ids and proof), on temporary workers permits, hbts, until legal inquiries are followed to determine status, 15-year residency if requested and paid for, after the inquiries, 3 years fast track after that.
* Speed up deportations of, criminal gang and drug members, drug carriers and terrorist only. They go to detention, judicial courts, and deportations. Nevertheless, make sure all legal rights are and due processes are met. Establish a reward system for innocence abroad scenarios. Moreover, all criminal abuses of immigrant are fully punished.

* Speed up conduct reviews. Increase training, regulation, and monitoring, ICE and all detention centers. Especially state based commercialized detentions centers require periodical, multiyear surprise auditing, as part of any JOB CREATION Federal Project. Even more frequent audits of state with historical questionable discriminatorily dedications.
* Falsely accused are entitled to reviews, civil action remedies, attorney presentation (Job creation).
* Increase training, regulation, and monitoring. Speed up conduct reviews. This is Job creation.
* No hide away judges, signature mass deportations, mistreatments, or deaths cover-ups or delays.
* Immediate access to medical, media, or attorneys as needed.

APPENDIX

D

Legal Notices

All Dr. Fakhraie's Fax, e-mails and open mails have an attached-legal note,
All Right Reserved & Other Legal Notes
G. Any and All Risks or Harms invokes these legal clauses. The Following legal clauses are base minimum, and will not limit all rights and legal protection, with uniform constitutional rights they are implied and accorded. Contractually all rights are implied and accorded. Please, read all the legal notes before using any materials. **G1**. In Cases of misuse of these materials, plagiarisms, use of computer identities to do harm, use to put at risk of harm, or to harm, (Legal, or etc.) the Firms, Trusts (FEDAT, FRDAT, All Entities), Dr. Bahman Fakhraie, His family members, will result in $60 million legal action per each event in United States Courts / any Jurisdictions determined or set by author or a trust set up by Dr. Bahman Fakhraie. There are added charges under ADA, ACA each. Also, use of creative ideas and intellectual properties for any commerce direct or indirect or by proxy, expansions of outlines, attempts to defraud, over charge, harm with illegal acts, misuse of private and confidential materials, information, and properties, letters, checks, e-mails, faxes, computers, all electronic devices, any and all communications, and any electronically stored materials and pictures, or false claims against the above entities will be an agreement with and subject to all elements of this contract, and as a use license, without nullifying further and ensuing legal actions or collections, or as directed by the same or authorities. All other contracts are one-time

contracts and s. t. this contract. Please, notify firm, Mr. Bahman Fakhraie, of all infractions, transactions, or transfer to individuals or to private or government entities in accord with current laws. **G2a**. All Costs due to inquiries, related or required business licenses, legal paper works and hours, all costs related to corrective or reparation publicity, bonding and insurances costs, stock related activities, all costs related to any harm (financial &legal) will be charged to the sources and inquirers, and none to the firm or Bahman Fakhraie, his family, or any and all of their related firms and assets. All attempts to harm, engagements, cashing checks or accepting cash from the same entities is an agreement with all elements of this contract. **G2b**. All copy rights associated with written works and further development of all works remains with the author Bahman Fakhraie or his trusts. All development rights are reserved by the same entities. **G3**. Any and all unsolicited commercial phone calls to Mr. Bahman Fakhraie, his family will result to a minimum of $500 per call charged to the source, due and payable in the same month the call is made, all other elements of this contract also apply, all contracts remain subservient to this contract, all costs of collection and legal actions also are added to the bill payable by source and not Bahman Fakhraie and these entities. **G4**. All Consultation and coaching involves risks due to market, business, political, etc. costs and damages related to all such risk are paid by individuals or business entities involved and none is implied or taken by Bahman Fakhraie, his family, or any related assets, under any and all conditions. These entities' court fees are $10,000, et minimum. **G5**. Uncomfortable conditions, misapplications of any law to harm, harassment, odd-hour calls, etc. will be due cause for termination of services without refund, and are actionable per this contract. §§§§

APPENDIX

E

Budgetary, Managerial Directives, and Legal Clauses

(Continue on next pages)

FERDT
FERDAT
FERDAT-C
Fakhraie Education Research Development And Trust Organization, Fakhraie Bahman
Grant proposal by
Bahman Fakhraie, PhD, ©, ®, ™

2011-01-22

Budgetary, Managerial Directive and Legal Clauses

Legal letter and charges for unauthorized information use.

Legal letter is in cases of e-fraud, misuse of firms' information, or harm under sec. G. All linked and relaying entities, institutions, governmental agencies are accountable no exception.

Dear Sirs, persons, INC., (illegal use of firms' info), your current bill is **$10,000, ≤Ceiling $60 mils.** On behalf of Dr. Bahman Fakhraie, FERDAT, and the firm, family, family trusts.
These are the current charges related to illegal e-fraud and all harmful misuse of firms' information, after the first time we asked you to terminate all contract and remove our name, firms' name etc. on this date.

1-Illegal use, the unapproved initial use of firm's name, contact name, duns #, any and all information supplied to USA government for the soul purpose of firm doing business with USA government, grant.gov, and NSF, Universities, other governmental and tribal entities, and all grantors. Minimum charges are $10,000.00, up to the ceiling of $ 60 million.

2-Use of firm contacts, names, address phone #, TIN/#s, and any information related to that.
Minimum charges are $10,000.00, up to the ceiling of $60 mils.

3- Continuation after repeated formal request to terminate illegal actions, sending junk e-mail, junk mail, forcing this firm to send back, by mail and certified mail. Legal costs related to that.
Minimum charges are $10,000.00 per each event, up to the ceiling of $60 mils.

4- Interference with firm soul business, time sensitive writing of government and private grants, at grant.gov, and NSF, universities, private foundations, NGOs and all grantors, with 4.5 million dollars floor. The Minimum charges are 4.5 million dollars, up to the ceiling of $60 mils.

4- Absolut or required non-disclosures by the firm or Dr. Fakhraie will require pre-paid plan with minimum flooring pay. Flex-legalism targeted at the firm, or Dr. B. Fakhraie will be due cause for nonpaid termination by the same, and harm-terms of Sec G of private contracts.

6- Punitive damages are up to 60 million dollars, if you do not stop, after the first notification.

Please make an effort to pay your bill. There will be additional charges added and sent to you for each time you try to contact the same entities, after the same dated termination notices.

Dr. BF, this is part of the legal notices under sec G.

Section 1, Mission Statement

To formulate optimum functionality in management teams, in order to make profitable and beneficial contributions, and create opportunity for merited advancements, **to advance research** in my fields of study. Utilizing rare combination of theory and empiricism, cultivated in multi-cultural inclusive settings in academic and private enterprises, I enhance the management in productivity and completion of productive projects, or suggest corrective recursive evaluation and total quality control improvements.

Experiences, among fields of International Trade, Managerial, and Production theories in Economics, Finance, Personal Finance management, and Businesses, which modern business and academic institutions find very expensive to employ and too costly not to employ. My extensive background help me advance research in my fields of study.

Section 2, Budgetary Clause

* All initial dedicated deposits (inflows) will be transferred to a FREDT, or FREDAT, FERDAT-C business account.

* No allotments or contracts activity will take place, until full transfer of funds has taken place per contracts. The cash-accounting method is used for tax purposes.

* *Alteration to submit to requirements and regulations will fully transfer all*

risks, fees, and penalties, and legal responsibilities, to the source of the requirements.

* There will be a minimum product list, or writing, or proposal-output for further research, which will be presented and agreed to at the initial phases.

* This will be the only output legally required at the end of contract, or at the end of grant periods.

* There is a managerial flow chart enclosed to enhance comprehensions of cash flow, read after the legal notes section.

Section 3, Managerial Clause

* Dr Bahman Fakhraie will act as agent, manger, and soul administrator, Executives director, Principle Investigator PI for FERDT, FERDAT, Fakhraie Bahman Organization, with full rights to take legal action and make final settlement on its accounts.

* Dr Bahman Fakhraie will act as agent, manger, and soul administrator for Fakhraie Bahman Organization, with

full right to take legal action on its accounts.

* A general electronic bookkeeping is followed, on periodical bases, as grants require it. Current standard is quarterly, post full disbursements of grant funding. (FRR is required quarterly)

* Details, information, managerial technologies are legally protected, and no such disclosure will be made of the Organization, administrator, assignees, or representatives of FERDT, FERDAT, or Fakhraie Bahman Organization. All copyright materials are marketable, or further developed by Mr. Fakhraie. All existing rights are reserved.

* All informal and formal requests can be made by mail, or email.

* There is forfeiture of all advances, in cases of mortality, health, or attempt at disbarment, legal action, harm, against soul administrator, Fakhraie Bahman Organization, with full right to take legal action on its accounts.

* Any and all such request will have to forward additional funding for legal representations and undue imposition of

costs or harm, please read the legal note and sec. G. It will always apply.

* *Alteration to submit to requirements and regulations will fully transfer all risks, fees, and penalties, and legal responsibilities, to the source of the requirements.*

* The reviewers will have access to a portion of the progress.

* Full transparencies are practiced for authorized agents only, mostly through the internet, after proper signatures are obtained.

* All future development, educational development will have to be contracted, or signed out temporarily.

* All copyrights and proprietary rights are reserved, granted, accorded to Dr Bahman Fakhraie, and his living trust.

* The final product in initial agreement will be shared with the grantors, after all the financial settlements have been met.

* PI, FERDAT; Fakhraie, Bahman

  Dr. Bahman Fakhraie, PhD, UOU, UT, USA

* Position Classification, Executive level I,

* Salary exceeds Fed Cap for private contracts.

* NSF ID, ████6796, Organizational ID Code, P ████8425

* Private for Profit Business:

* DUNS Number D&B # ████9684,

* CAGE/NCAGE: ███S3, Congressional Districts, UT_001

* Sec G of private contract always applies

* For institutional DUNS, etc. Please, check cover letter, or contact PI. Thanks

* UOU PI Information

□ Federal Interagency Committee on Education (FICE) Code for the U: **003675**
□ EIN. TAX ID/TIN: **87-[redacted]0525**
□ DUNS Num: **D & B #[redacted]95365**
□ Cage Code: **3T 624**
□ NSF Institutional Code: **[redacted]56000**
□ NIH Institutional Code: **[redacted]002**
□ Congressional District: **UT-002**
□ Type of Organization: **State Institution of Higher Education**
□ AAALAC Accreditation: **8 March 2000 - (Animal Resource Center Facilities and Programs Accreditation)**
□ USDA Registration Number (Animal Subject): **87-R-0001**
□ PHS Animal Welfare Assurance ID Number: **A3031-01**
□ Human Subjects Federal Wide Assurance: **[redacted]00003745 (expires 11.06.2011)**
□ Effective Date of Cost Accounting Statement: **Disclosure Statement submitted 12.31.97 (not yet audited or approved by**
* **DHHS)**

Section 4, Legal Clause, All Right Reserved & Other Legal Notes

E. Speech, Lecture Tours, and Research Papers & Follow Up:

All publications or Grant-products are commonly published on completion, USA Library of Congress, Trade Journals, Or Author's websites, etc.

Contact for individualized contracts

F. For Time Donation, And Charity Events: 1. 5% of Net contracts paid 2. Time By Appointments Only.3. Write Donations Checks to: Fakhraie Trust fund / Bahman Fakhraie

G. Any and All Risks or Harms invokes these legal clauses. The Following legal clauses are base minimum, and will not limit all rights and legal protection, with uniform constitutional rights they are implied and accorded. Contractually all rights are implied and accorded. Please, read all the legal notes before using any materials.

G1. In Cases of misuse of these materials, plagiarisms, use to put at risk of harm, or to harm, (Legal, or Etc.) the firm, CEO, FERDT, president: Mr. Bahman Fakhraie, His family members, it will result in $60 million legal action per each event in United States Courts/ any Jurisdictions determined or set by author or a trust set up by Mr. Bahman Fakhraie. Also, use of creative ideas and intellectual properties for any commerce direct or indirect or by proxy, expansions of outlines, attempts to defraud, over charge, harm with illegal acts, misuse of private and confidential materials, information, and properties, letters, checks, e-mails, faxes, any and all communications, and any electronically stored materials and pictures, or false claims against the above entities will be an agreement with and subject to all elements of this contract, and as a user license, without nullifying further and ensuing legal actions or collections, or as directed by the same or authorities. All other contracts are one time contracts and s. t. this contract. Please, notify firm, Mr. Bahman Fakhraie, of all infractions, transactions, or transfer to individuals or to private or government entities in accord with current laws.

G2a. All Costs due to inquiries, related or required business licenses, legal paper works, and hours, all costs related to corrective or reparation publicity, bonding and insurances costs, stock related activities, all costs related to any harm (financial & legal) will be charges to the sources and inquirers, and none to the firm or Bahman

Fakhraie, his family, or any and all of their related assets. All attempts to harm, engagements, cashing checks or accepting cash from the same entities is an agreement with all elements of this contract.

G2b. All copy rights associated with written works and further development of all works remains with the author Bahman Fakhraie or his trusts. All development rights are reserved by the same entities.

G3. Any and all unsolicited commercial phone calls, to Mr. Bahman Fakhraie and, his family will result to a minimum of $ 500 per call charged to the source, due and payable in the same month the call is made, all other elements of this contract also apply, all contracts remain subservient to this contract, all costs of collection and legal actions also are added to the bill payable by source and not Bahman Fakhraie and these entities.

G4. All Consultation and coaching involves risks due to market, business, political, etc. costs and damages related to all such risk are paid by individuals or business entities involved and none is implied or taken by Bahman Fakhraie, his family, or any related assets, under any and all conditions. These entities' court fees are $10,000; et minimum.

G5. Uncomfortable conditions, misapplications of any law to harm, harassment, odd-hour calls, etc will be due cause for termination of services without refund, and are actionable per this contract.

§§§§

All Right Reserved & Other Legal Notes

All publications or Grant-products are published on completion, USA Library of Congress, Trade Journals, Or Author's websites, etc.

E. Speech, Lecture Tours, Research Papers & Follow Up:

1. Per Each Event-$ 350,000 +.
2. with Foreign Travel-$ 3,000,000
3. Book/Cash Advance $6,000,000; Net Royalties ∃40%
4. Scripts: /Starting from....................$ 300,000
5. Movie Script (120+Pages)................$ 3,000,000
6. Or Cash Advance Plus 2% of All Gross paid annually
7. Consultations Fee/Initial charge non-refunded $ 10,000, & ...10 %
8. Business limited ventures, partnerships, etc. .... ∃ 30%
9. Salary executive level I, Fed cap for fed grants, higher for privates.

F. For Time Donation, And Charity Events: 1. 5% of Net contracts paid 2. Time By Appointments Only.3. Write Donations Checks to Fakhraie Trust fund / Bahman Fakhraie. G. Any and All Risks or Harms invokes these legal clauses. The Following legal clauses are base minimum, and will not limit all rights and legal protection, with uniform constitutional rights they are implied and accorded. Contractually all rights are implied and accorded. Please, read all the legal notes before using any materials. G1. In Cases of misuse of these materials, plagiarisms, use to put at risk of harm, or to harm, (Legal, or Etc.) the firm, CEO: Mr. Bahman Fakhraie, His family members, will result in $60 million legal action per each event in United States Courts/Jurisdictions determine by author or a trust set up by Mr. Bahman Fakhraie. Also, use of creative ideas intellectual properties, expansions of outlines, attempts to defraud, over charge, harm with illegal acts, misuse of private and confidential materials and properties, letters, e-mails, faxes, any and all communications, and any electronically stored materials and pictures, or false claims against the above entities will be an agreement with all elements of this contract, and as a use license, without nullifying ensuing legal actions or collections, or as directed by the same or authorities. Please, notify firm, Mr. Bahman Fakhraie, of any and all infractions, transactions, or transfer to individuals or to private or government entities. G2a. All Costs due to inquiries, related or required business licenses, legal paper works and hours, all costs related to corrective or reparation publicity, bonding and insurances costs, stock related activities, all costs related to any harm (financial & legal) will be charges to the sources and inquirers, and none to the firm or Bahman Fakhraie, his family, or any and all of their related assets. All attempts to harm, engagements, cashing checks or accepting cash from the same entities is an agreement with all elements of this contract. G2b. All copy rights associated with written works and further development of all works remains with the author Bahman Fakhraie or his trusts. Any and all development rights are reserved by the same entities. G3. Any and all unsolicited commercial phone calls to Mr. Bahman Fakhraie, his family will result to a minimum of $ 500 per call charged to the source, due and payable in the same month the call is made, all other elements of this contract also apply, all contracts remain subservient to this contract, all costs of collection and legal actions also are added to the bill payable by source and not Bahman Fakhraie and these entities. G4. All Consultation and coaching involves risks due to market, business, political, etc. costs and damages related to all such risk are paid by individuals or business entities involved and none is implied or taken by Bahman Fakhraie, his family, or any related assets, under any and all conditions. These entities' court fees are $10,000; et minimum. G5. Uncomfortable conditions, misapplications of any law to harm, harassment, odd-hour calls, etc will be due cause for termination of services without refund, and are actionable per this contract.

§§§§

Letter of Agreement with FRDET FREDAT< FERDAT-C and Fakhraie Bahman

I/We (Ms, Mrs, Mr): ....

Business Name: ....

Social Security numbers: ..../......./................ ..../......./................

Tax ID Numbers: ....

Driver License Numbers: ....

Passport (Birth Certificate) Numbers ....

Have read all the information supplied by Mr Bahman Fakhraie, and /or FRDET (Trust, LLP). Agree to supply all correct financial and related information and select the following services by marking (X), or Letter a b c, Or Number 1 2 3, or write and specify. Agree to the power of attorney required to confirm or acquire financial and related information. Plus a check for $3000, for preliminary registrations, legal and financial inquiries, and licensing fees.

1: □ 2: □ 3: □ 4: □ 5: □ 6: □ 7: □ 8: □

Specify which kinds of the following accounts you will require:

Individual/Gov. □ Joints □ Joint with survival rights □ Trusts □

Details: ....

Business types:

Ltd Partnership (LLP, LLC) □ Soul Owner □ Inc/Gov □ Firm □

Details: ....

I/We agree to pay the fees and costs as they accrue, after 30 days a charge of %10 per annum is added to past due amounts until they are settled or paid in full. That at least 75% charges and expenses are paid no later than six month after initial reports or outlines are examined. That all travel lodgings and phone charges, legal research, and research hours, I/We request are fully paid. I/We have read and understand the nature of business, business cycles, market price fluctuation risks, currency fluctuation risks, social and political risks, natural and climatic risks, and all other risks herewith not itemized; therefore, I/we accept all financial losses, responsibilities, all punitive or compensatory damages that occur for all activities that are undertaken based on or claimed related to the report or reports, advise and etc., generated by Money Wise Firm, Bahman Fakhraie or all the entities named, agents, and associates. I/We understand in cases of any false, misleading, or withholding information the Money Wise Firm and all entities named above will not be held accountable, responsible, financially or otherwise, and will be refunded for any damages fully. I/We release all others associated with Money Wise Firm, and Bahman Fakhraie from financial losses, responsibilities, all compensatory and punitive charges concerning activities I/We undertake.

Sign (full name, titles, and address)

Business (Name, Address; Agents' title):

Section 5, Organization Chart

⇔Requests for grants, grant and contract proposals and Minimums contracted output Grant Funds,

⇓ Organization DUNS, University DUNS ⇓

Administrator ⇒FRDAT

⇓

FERDAT
& FERDAT-C
Research, Publishing, and Production
President, Administrator, Executive level 1
⇓

Bahman Fakhraie, PhD, © 2011, UOU, UT, USA
®, ™

⇓

Tasks and controls, TQC, and Redo, Recycles

⇔Tax and expense disbursements

⇓

Completed project Vs. Minimums contracted output

⇔ Informal notification of source of funds, with future project proposal if any,

⇒Formal and final notification from FRDET, FERDAT

⇔ Final confirmation of conclusion from Administrators

⇒ Final confirmation of conclusion from Organization Fakhraie

⇔ Keeping communication and network open to future project

(All illegal activities are promptly reported)

Bahman Fakhraie, PhD, © ® ™ 2010-, UOU, UT, USA

Section 6, DATA MANAGEMENT:

Relevant data will be managed, and stored.

Moreover, the data and the progression of data used will be stored post completion.

As a common practice, Dr Bahman Fakhraie will, also preserve a historical over view of data for legal purposes, for future use. A portion of that will be shared if requested in written form, post settlement of all expenses.

The ethical requirements will be followed in accordance with the applied law established.

The final product will be shared with the grantors, after all the financial settlements have been met. The reviewers will have access to a portion of the progress.

All publications or Grant-products are published on completion, USA Library of Congress, Trade Journals, FERDAT Publishing, Or Author's websites, etc.

Labor laws and benefit distribution will be according to the institutional Fed Cap limits, private contracts; vendors are responsible for their own legal obligations. (Publication Ink, FedExx, kinkcos, vendors etc.)

CPA and Legal establishment, outside to this entity will be contracted to handle more complex issues when they arise, all cost are due, prior to any such required actions are requested.

Full transparencies are practiced for authorized agents only, mostly through the internet, after proper signatures are obtained. All copyrights and proprietary rights are granted, accorded and reserved to Dr Bahman Fakhraie,

All future development, educational development will have to be contracted, or signed out temporarily, they will revert to Dr. Bahman Fakhraie, in case of any and all legal issues.

These and other clauses will be amended and upgraded as required over time, they all apply.

Absolut or required non-disclosures by the firm or Dr. Fakhraie will require pre-paid plan with minimum flooring pay. Flex-legalism targeted at the firm, or Dr. B. Fakhraie will be due cause for nonpaid termination by the same.

G. Any and All Risks or Harms invokes these legal clauses. The Following legal clauses are base minimum, and will not limit all rights and legal protection, with uniform constitutional rights they are implied and accorded. Contractually all rights are implied and accorded. Please, read all the legal notes before using any materials.

Section 7, Vita

Bahman Fakhraie, PH.D. University Of Utah
Economic Dept., Salt Lake City, Utah USA, 84112
Permanent Address: c/o 1120 Canyon Rd #29; Ogden Utah 84404-7663
E-Mail: bf9@utah.edu , dr.bahf.econ@gmail.com

Honors and Awards: Omicron Delta Epsilon Honor Society

Student leadership positions: President of International Student Association

Bachelor of Science: Utah State University

Master of Science: Utah State University

PhD, University of Utah University of Utah

Mission Statement:

To formulate optimum functionality in management teams, in order to make profitable and beneficial contributions, and create opportunity for merited advancements.

Utilizing rare combination of theory and empiricism, cultivated in multi-cultural inclusive settings in academic and private enterprise, I enhance the management in productivity and completion of productive projects, or suggest corrective recursive evaluation and total quality control improvements.

Experiences, among fields of International Trade, Managerial, and Production theories in Economics, Finance, Personal Finance and Business, which modern business and academic institutions find very expensive to employ and too costly not to employ. The extensive background helps advance research in my fields of study.

Goals:

I have initiated, passed, and funded many constructive projects -- goals by committees--, where it has been value enhancing and mutually beneficial individually, and by team assists.

Private Senior Economist: Research Positions with Contracts, Teaching, Research, Books, with contract.

Short Term Private Contracts are for economic and financial educational consultations.

Academic Preparatory Continuum:

PhD, University of Utah

Dissertation: TECHNOLOGICAL INJECTION, DYNAMIC NEW CAPITAL MEASUREMENTS, AND PRODUCTION THEORY IN ECONOMICS

Dr. Bahman Fakhraie's Book-link is at, https://order.proquest.com/OA_HTML/pqdtibeCCtpItmDspRte.jsp

Thesis statement:

The dynamic influences of technology and elemental factors of production --defined and measured in this dissertation-- are greater than commonly have been calculated or expected. The impacts of different measurements of capital stocks (traditional and new adjusted capital) on embodied and disembodied technological variables, on productivity, and economic growth of national social products are tested. The econometric effects of two new capital stock measures introduced in the writing of Friedrich August Von Hayek, John Maynard Keynes, and further developed by Evsey D. Domar, and ignored by most modern economists are examined. Therefore, we focus on the demand and supply side of technological embodied in capital, in human skill and produced goods and services, and the economy.

Post-Doctoral Goals:

1. Updating the econometrics of the dissertation to most recent available data and dates. (per available grants)

2. Include, countries, with acceptable data in the study, set up formulaic development in excel etc for use.(per grants)

3. Focus on the theoretical advancement in production processes for systemic innovational additive methodologies, in Movie production, Agriculture, and other creative industries, using existing or newly hired faculties, in anchored and linked institutions. This is a great serious work in shadows of Adam Smith, Schumpeter, Hayak, and Keynes.

4. Stream line methodologies, and project for PhD Students, master students, and introductory fields' level, an extension of the dissertation and current copyrighted writings.

5. Of course, this will be under Sec G of private contract and without infringing on rights of marketing, publishing, and distribution of the same. Certain contracts will be more restrictive, including specific names.

Production theory in Agriculture

Agro-production, Sheep production in Iran (an onsite research project 1975)

Monetary Macroeconomic Specialization (Milton Freedman,)

International Monetary macroeconomic Specializations (Robert Mundell)

Fiscal Analysis of oscillatory modifications

Applied Agricultural production in developing economies

Inappropriate Technology Transfers by Corporations

and dualistic induced instabilities in a pre-democratic economies.

SELECTED BIBLIOGRAPHY

Bailey, Martin J., *National Income and the Price Level: A Study in Macroeconomic Theory,* New York: McGraw-Hill, 1971.

Baumol, William J., *Economic Theory and Operational Analysis,* 4th ed., New Jersey: Prentice-Hall, 1977.

Blaug, Mark., *Economic Theory in Retrospect,* 3rd Ed., London: The Cambridge University Press, 1978.

Böhn_Bawerk, Eugen Von., *Capital and Interest: Positive Theory of Capital,* vol. II, Trans. G. D. Hunt & H. F. Sennholz, Chicago: Libertarian Press, 1959.

Boulding, Kenneth E., *Economics As A science*, New York: McGraw-Hill Book Company, 1970.

Byers, Lloyd L., *Concept of Strategic Management: Planning and Implementation*, New York: Harper & Row Publishers.

Caves, Richard E. and Jones, R. W., *World Trade and Payments: An Introduction*, 2nd ed., Boston: Little, Brown and Company, 1977.

Chiang, Alpha C., *Fundamental Methods of Mathematical Economics*, 2nd ed., New York: McGraw-Hill Book Company, 1974.

Coombs, Philip H., *The World Educational Crisis: A System Analysis*, London: Oxford University Press, 1968.

Domar, Evsey D., *Essays in the Theory of Economic Growth*, New York: Oxford University Press, 1957, 154-167, 168, 181.

Druker, Peter F., *Innovation and Entrepreneurship*, New York: Harper & Row Publishers, 1985.

Eisner, R. "Depreciation Allowances, Replacement Requirement, and Growth," *The American Economic Review*, XLII, December 1952.

Fakhraie, Bahman, *Technological injection, dynamic new capital measurements, and Production Theory in Economics*, (Michigan: ProQuest LLC, 2010) an, https://order.proquest.com/OA_HTML/pqdtibeCCtpItmDspRte.jsp

—, *Analytical Remedies for The Millennial Cascading Economics declines,* Utah, FERDAT Publishing, 2012

—, *The Demand and Supply Sides of Appropriate Technological Advancement,* Utah, FERDAT Publishing,

2012

—, *TECONOMICS, The Microeconomic Analysis*, Scientific Synthesis of Microeconomics, mathematics and statistical methodologies and technological parameters in production, Utah, FERDAT publishing, 2012

—. "The Demand and Supply Sides of Appropriate Technological Advancement," (Research paper at University of Utah Economics Dept. 2003)

—. "Economic Theories and Practices in Technological Changes, capital measures, and Production." (Research paper at University of Utah Economics Dept. 1988)

—. "Hallowing headless nations: the need to invest on public education under the 1980s international economic conditions," (Research paper at University of Utah Economics Dept. 1988)

—. "Transfer of Technologies and Socioeconomic Theories of Dualism," (Research paper at University of Utah Economics Dept. 1983)

Fellner, William J., *Competition Among the Few*, New York, Augustus m. Kelley Publisher, 1965

Friedman, Milton and Schwartz, Anna Jacobson, *The Great Contraction 1929-1933*, vol.2, 2nd ed., New Jersey: Princeton University Press, 1973

Gander, James Patrick., *Technological Change and Raw Materials*, Salt Lake City: Bureau of Economic and Business Research, University of Utah, 1977.

Gardner, Ackley, *Macroeconomics: Theory and Policy*, New York: Macmillan Publishing Co., 1978.

Girton, Lance and Roper Don, "Theory and Implication of Currency Substitution," *Journal of Money, Credit, and Banking,* 13, no. 1 (February 1981): 12-30.

Hayek, Friedrich August Von., "Kapitalaufzehrung." Weltwirtschaftliches Archive 36, 1932, II, 86-108.

Heilbroner, Robert L., *The Worldly Philosophers*, New York: Time Inc., Special Ed., 1962.

Hicks, Sir John, *The Crisis in Keynesian Economics*, New York: Basic Books, Inc. 1974.

Hirshleifer, Jack, *Investment, Interest, and Capital*, New Jersey: Prentice-Hall, 1970.

—. *Time, Uncertainty, and Information*, New York: Basil Blackwell, 1989.

—. *Price Theory and Applications*, New Jersey: Prentice-Hall, 1976.

Henderson, J. M. and Quandt, R. E., *Microeconomic Theory; A Mathematical Approach*, 2nd ed., New York: McGraw-Hill, 1972. 191-199, 280

Hunt, E. K. and Howard J. Sherman, Economics*: An Introduction to Traditional and Radical Views*, 2nd Ed., San Francisco: Harper and Row Publishers, 1975.

Intriligator, Michael D., *Econometric Models, Techniques, and Applications*, New Jersey: Prentice-Hall, 1978.

Johnson, J., *Econometric Methods*. New York: McGraw-Hill, 1972.

Kant, Immanuel, *Critique of Judgment*, Trans. J. H. Bernard, New York: Hafner, 1951.

Kennedy Charles and Thirlwall, A.P., "Surveys in Applied Economics: Technological Progress," *The Economic Journal*, March 1972: 12.

Keynes, John Maynard, *Essays in Biography*, London: The Cambridge University Printing House for Royal Economic Society, 1972.

—. *The General Theory of Employment, Interest and Money,* 1st ed. 1936, London: The Cambridge University Printing House for Royal Economic Society, Reprint 1973.

Kindleberger, Charles P., *The World in Depression 1929-1939*, Los Angeles: University of California Press, 1973.

Kirzner, I.M., *Discovery and the Capitalist Process*, Chicago: University of Chicago Press, 1985.

Klein, P. A. and Moore, G. H., *Monitoring Growth Cycles in Market-Oriented Countries*, (Mass.: published for N. B. E. R., by Ballinger publishing Co., 1985).

Knight, Farnk H., *Risk, Uncertainty and Profit*, Chicago: University of Chicago Press, 1985.

Landes, David S., *The wealth and poverty of nations: Why Some are So Rich and Some are So Poor*, (New York: W.W. Norton & Company, 1998).

Lindert, Peter H. and Kindleberger Charles P., *International Economics,* 7th Ed., Illinois: Richard Irwin, 1982.

Mansfield, Edwin, *Technological Change*, New York: W. W. Norton & Co., 1971.

Mark, Blaug, *Economic Theory in Retrospect*, 3rd Ed. London: The Cambridge University Press, 1978.

Marx, K. (In a letter he wrote to Engel, dated 20 August, 1862, London), (handout by Professor Randa, 2004)

McKinnon, Ronald I., *Money and Capital in Economic Development*, Washington D. C.: The Brookings Institution, 1973.

Mensch, Gerhard, Das *technilogische Patt*., Frankfurt: Umschau Verlag, 1975.

—, *Stalemate in Technology: innovation overcome the Depression*, (Massachusetts: Ballinger Publishing Company, 1979).

Miles, T.R., "Gestalt Theory," in The Encyclopedia of Philosophy, New York: Macmillan Publishing Co., vols. 3 and 4, 1967.

Mishan, Edward Joshua, *Cost-Benefit Analysis,* 4th Ed. London: Unwin Hyman, 1988.

Moran, Michael. "New England Transcendentalism," in The Encyclopedia of Philosophy, (New York: Macmillan Publishing Co., Vols. 3 and 4, 1967).

Mundell, Robert A. , "Growth, Stability, and Inflationary Finance," Journal *of Political Economy*, 73, 1963.

Pindyck, R.S., and Rubinfeld, D.L., *Econometric Models and Econometric*, 2nd ed., New York: McGraw-Hills, 1981.

Ott, J. Steven, *The Organizational Culture Perspectives*, (Pacific Grove, California: Brooks/Cole Publishing Company, 1989).

Quirk, James and Saposnik, Rubin, *Introduction to General Equilibrium Theory and Welfare Economics*, New York: McGraw-Hill, 1968.

Rima, Ingrid, *Development of Economic Analysis*, 7th ed., New York: Routledge, 2009.

Rodinson, M., *Islam and Capitalism*, Trans. B. Pearce, Austin: University of Texas, 1981.

Rosenberg, Nathan, Technology *and American Economic Growth*, New York: M. E. Sharp, 1972.

Ruttan, V. W. , "Usher and Schumpeter on Invention, and Technological Change," Quarterly *Journal of Economics*, 1960, 602.

Ruttan, Vernon W. , "Usher and Schumpeter on Invention, Innovation, and Technological change," Quarterly *Journal of Economics*, 1960, 73.

Samuelson, Anthony Paul. Economics, 11th Ed., New York: McGraw-Hill, 1980.

Savich, R.S., and Thomson, L. A., *Resource Allocation within the Product Life Cycles*, Business Topic, MSU: MSU, fall 1978.

Schmooker, Jacob, *Invention and Economic Growth*, Massachusetts: Harvard University Press, 1966.

Schultz, Theodore W. , *Investing in People: The Economics of Population Quality*, Berkley: University of California Press, 1982.

Schumpeter, Joseph A., *Business Cycles*, vol. 1. New York: McGraw Hill Book Company, 1939.

—. *Business Cycles: A Theoretical, Historical, and Statistical Analysis of the Capitalists Process,* vol. I, New York: McGraw Hill Book Company, 1938.

—. *The Theory of Economic Development: An Inquiry into Profits, Capital, Credit, Interest, and Business Cycle*, Trans., Redvers Opie, London: Oxford University Press, Reprint 1980.

Smith, Adam., *An Inquiry into the Nature and Cause of Wealth of Nations*, Edited by E. Cannon, Chicago: University of Chicago Press, 1976.

—. *An Inquiry into the Nature and Causes of Wealth of Nations*, vol. 2, 2nd ed., Oxford: the Clarendon Press, 1988.

—. *The Theory of Moral Sentiments*, London, 1st ed., 1757.

Smith, E.J. Chambers, R.H. Scott and R.S., *National Income Analysis and Forecasting*, Glenview: Scott, Foresman and Company, 1975.

Spiegle, Henry William., *The Growth of Economic thought*, North Carolina: Duke University Press, 1983.

Stigler, George J., *The Theory of Price*, 3rd ed., New York: The Macmillan Company, 1966.

Takaki, Ronald., *A Different Mirror: A History of Multicultural America*, London: Little Brown and Company, 1993.

Taylor, John R., *An Introduction to Error Analysis*, Mill Valley: University Science Books, 1982.

Thirtle, Colin G. and Ruttan V. W., *The Role of Demand and Supply in the Generation of Diffusion of Technological Change*, Switzerland, 1987.

U. S. President, *Economic Report of the President*, (Washington, D.C.: Government printing office, 1990)

Usher, Abbot Payson, *A History of Mechanical Inventions*, London: Oxford University Press, 1954.

Usher, Abbot Payson, *A History of Mechanical Inventions,* Revised ed., London: Oxford University Press, 1954.

Viner, Jacob, *Studies in the Theories of International Trade*, New York: Harper and Brothers publishers, 1937.

Wainwright, A. C. Chiang and K., *Fundamental Methods of Mathematical Economics*, 4th ed., Boston: McGraw-Hill Irwin, 2005.

Webster, Merriam, *Merriam-Webster's Collegiate Dictionary*, 9th ed., Springfield: M.W. Inc., 1985.

Young, Hugh D., *Statistical Treatment of Experimental Data*, New York: McGraw-Hill, 1962.

ACADEMIC VITA

Bahman Fakhraie, PhD University of Utah, United State of America, and Major Fields of studies are in international trade and finance, supporting fields are in Development economics, urban economics, production theory and agronomy. Master of Science is in Agricultural Economics from Utah State University. Major Field is Production theory in economics, Mathematic economics, Development theory, Macroeconomics backgrounds. Bachelor of Science is in Agronomy, which is the applied, empirical optimum production in Agricultural production. Dr. Bahman Fakhraie is a well-trained economist. He is an empiricists and theoretician with extensive written background. He is a private contractor and real estate investor. He also has backgrounds in university classroom teaching.

Mission Statement: To formulate optimum functionality in management teams, in order to make profitable and beneficial contributions, and create opportunity for merited advancements. Utilizing rare combination of theory and empiricism, cultivated in multi-cultural inclusive settings in academic and private enterprise, I enhance the management in productivity and completion of productive projects, or suggest corrective recursive evaluation and total quality control improvements.

Experiences, among fields of International Trade, Managerial, and Production theories in Economics, Finance, Personal Finance and Business, Rural and Urban development, which modern businesses and academic institutions find very expensive to employ and too costly not to employ. The extensive background helps advance research in my fields of studies.

Goals: I have initiated, passed, and funded many constructive projects --goals by committees-- where it has been value enhancing and mutually beneficial individually, and by team assists. Private Senior Economist: Research Positions with Contracts, Teaching, Research, Books, with contract. Short Term Private Contracts are for economic and financial educational consultations.

Dr. Bahman Fakhraie came for education to USU, based on friendships forged since world war two, between his father and Senator Frank M. Browning and an invitation to study at Utah State University. He has been a touchstone in many students' and family members' academic-lives, with masters and PhDs of their own. Dr. Bahman Fakhraie served as the president of International Student Association, during his undergraduate years at Utah State University. Dr. Fakhraie and President Glen L. Taggart invited Ambassador Ardeshir Zahedi of Iran to celebrate Iranian New Year (Nurooz), with the university community. His master studies included an on-site study of Agricultural production in Khuzestan, Islamic republic of Iran 1975.

He married Kay Davis, a USU alumnus with her master in Speech Pathology. She has contributed diligently to the children in her field. Daughter, Miss Lara Fatemeh Fakhraie earned her Master degree from Oregon State University. She is an author and an editor and publishers of an insightful Blog. Son, Mr. Anayat Wayne Fakhraie has a Screenwriter's master of fine art from American Film Institute with experience and contributions in his field.

Dr. Bahman Fakhraie, has published his dissertation," Technological Injection, Dynamic New capital Measurements and Production Theory in Economics," Dr. Fakhraie's Book-link is at, https://order.proquest.com/OA_HTML/pqdtibeCCtpItmDspRte.jsp

The impacts of different measurements of capital stocks (traditional and new adjusted capital) on embodied and disembodied technological variables, on productivity, and economic growth of national social products are tested. The econometric effects of two new capital stock measures introduced in the writing of Friedrich August Von Hayek, John Maynard Keynes, and further developed by Evsey D. Domar, and ignored by most modern economists are examined. Therefore, we focus on the demand and supply side of technological embodied in capital, in human skill and produced goods and services, and the economy.

Post-Doctoral Goals:

6. Apply most recent updated data to update the econometrics of the dissertation. (per available grants)

7. Include, countries, with acceptable data in the study, set up formulaic development in excel etc. for use.(per grants)

8. Focus on the theoretical advancement in production processes for systemic innovational additive methodologies, in Movie production, Agriculture, manufacturing, and other new and creative industries, using existing or newly hired faculties, in anchored and linked institutions. This is a great serious work in shadows of Adam Smith, Schumpeter, Hayak, and Keynes.

9. Stream line methodologies, and project for PhD Students, master students, and introductory fields' level, an extension of the dissertation and current copyrighted writings.

10. Apply for optimum employment in specialization fields of studies.

11. Of course, this will be under Sec G of private contract and without infringing on rights of marketing, publishing, and distribution of the same. Certain contracts will be more restrictive, including specific names.

He is editing two new books for publishing in his field. He is grateful to his knowledgeable extended family, friends, and professors globally.

BIOGRAPHY

Dr. Bahman Fakhraie, PhD, Economics, University of Utah, Salt Lake City Utah, BS, and MS from Utah State University, at Logan Utah. Dr. Bahman Fakhraie dissertation adds to the influences and importance of the Unorthodox-Holistic Economic analyses, or the Gestalt of Unorthodox economic doctrine, in the millennial age of technological paradigm shifts. He applies analytical and research skills with a holistic view of events, history, mathematics, and econometrics to economic analysis, with scientific background and multimedia digitized presentations for marketing. He is A Published Economist, Author, Researcher, Investor, and Private Contractor. His expertise are in international trade and finance, economic production, growth (theory and application), development theory, econometrics, (math, micro, and macro), Agriculture economics, and agronomy.

He grew up working in family businesses, banking, small farm, mechanic shop, auto shop. Bookkeeping, salesperson, clerk, heavy machine operator, truck and tractor driver, and construction, shop booker and manager, customer service, billing and complain department, with many good uplifting stories. He experienced forest and water conservation, pest and weed management, herd management and control, game managements and control, agricultural land and soil reclamation, preservation, and crop production first hand. Dr. Bahman Fakhraie was invited by Senator Frank M. Browning of Bank of Utah Ogden Utah to attend Utah State University, when Senator

Browning visited his family. He already had met Dr. and Mrs. Pollard, and Dr. and Mrs. Call of USU Logan Utah, while they were doing agricultural and development research in Iran. In memoriam all great and dear people, their great work is appreciated. Also Mr. and Mrs. Ward with Steve and Barbara live in Hawaii. During his under graduate work at USU, he serviced as the president of foreign student association. He enjoyed, and maintains leadership trainings and managerial skills. President of Utah State University Glenn L. Taggart and Dr. Bahman Fakhraie invited Iranian Ambassador Adeshir Zahedi, and world-renowned Iranian entertainers for Nurooz. Mr. Ambassador donated substantially to the University. After earning a Bachelor and a Master's degree at Utah State University, he continued his education at University of Utah. You can study his publications on internet, as they are available and updated.

In the summer of 1976, Bahman married Kay Davis, a USU student studying for her master in Speech Pathology. She has earned her master, certificates, and licenses. She is contributing greatly to the children of State in her field. They raised two University of Utah Alumni, his son and daughter. They have achieved success in their fields. His daughter, Miss Lara Fatemeh Fakhraie, earned her Master's degree from Oregon State University and is now a published author. She resides in Oregon. His son, Mr. Anayat Wayne Fakhraie, received his Master's degree from the American Film Institute as a screenwriter. He has an agent, and he is developing material for several production companies and resides in Los Angeles California. Dr. Fakhraie families have endured multiple revolutions, departure of many family members, and hardships in their academic journey. The caravan of joy de vive, never a Sui juries, carries on.

I would like to thank Dr. Lance Girton, the chair of my supervisory committee, and Dr. Peter W. Philips, the chair of the Economics department at the University of Utah, and professors Stephen Reynolds, James Patrick Gander, and J. Steven Ott, all distinguished members of my supervisory committee. Special thanks to Dr. S. H. Rokni, world-renowned nuclear physics specialist at SLAC Stanford University, Dr. Hamid Fakhraei. I am grateful to Professors E. K. Hunt, Korkut Alp Erturk, and David M. Kiefer, previous economic department heads. I thank Dr. Khosrow Mostofi, then Director of the UOU Middle East Center, Dr. James Kritzeck, Directors of Graduate Studies, Dr. Hussein Fahim, the department of Anthropology, and Mrs. Lucille Seely, Graduate Fellowships, for their support. I thank Dr. Haideh Salehi, Dr. Robert R. Edminster, and Dr. Lawrence Nabors. In memoriam, I am grateful for the extended conversations and tea, and friendship of the rare scholar, late professor Ernest William Randa. University of Utah President David W. Pershing, and past president Michael K. Young, Social and Behavioral Sciences Dean M. David Rudd, Graduate school Dean White, and his team, Economic Department Chair Thomas Neil Maloney, Dr. Bahman Bakhtiari, UOU ME Dept. chair. I thank the UOU Graduate School Thesis (and assists) editors, CHRISTINE PICKETT, MARTHA KLEIN, and Kelly Harward. I also thank Mary R. Guillory and Tracey Anne Farnsworth at Economic Department, and Michelle Hymer, Darci Berg, Sandy Haughtey, and the staff of Dean Charles E. Wight, at the University Of Utah Graduate School.

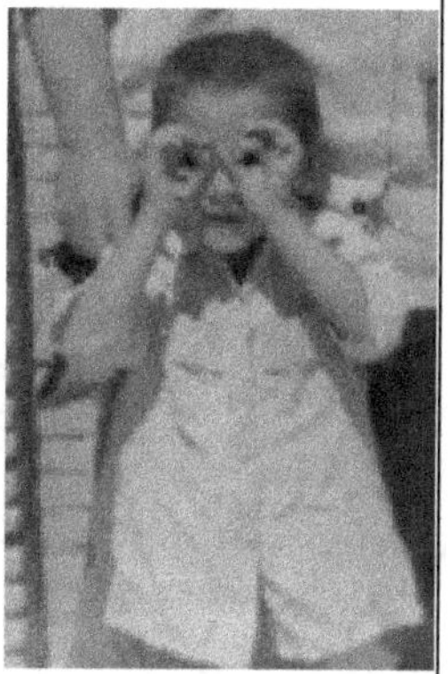

Dr. Bahman Fakhraie wrote his dissertation on "*Technological Injection, Dynamic New Capital Measurements and Production theory in Economics*." His studies are globally renowned, and he contributes to his field by book publications and post-doctoral research. Dr. Bahman Fakhraie hopes to further contribute to his field and assist with educational causes. His research on technological advancements and new measures of capital, and capital formation yielded three books, already globally renowned. Dr. Bahman Fakhraie is very grateful to family, friends, professors, around the world.

*** © ***

New books,
Technological Injection, Dynamic New Capital Measurements and Production theory in Economics,
https://order.proquest.com/OA_HTML/pqdtibeCCtpItmDspRte.jsp

TECONOMIC ANALYSIS, ANALYTICAL ECONOMIC REMEDIES FOR THE POST-CRASH MILLENNIAL ECONOMIES

THE DEMAND AND SUPPLY SIDES OF APPROPRIATE TECHNOLOGICAL ADVANCEMENT

TECONOMICS, THE MICROECONOIC ANALYSIS, Scientific Synthesis of Microeconomics, mathematics and statistical
methodologies and technological parameters in production in Teconomics

Others on the WEB pages of Dr. Bahman Fakhraie, PHD.

http://drbahfecon.wixsite.com/teconomics

https://www.amazon.com/Dr.-Bahman-Fakhraie/e/B00IKAR1CM/ref=ntt_athr_dp_pel_1%20https://www.createspace.com/4703954

BOOK PROMO

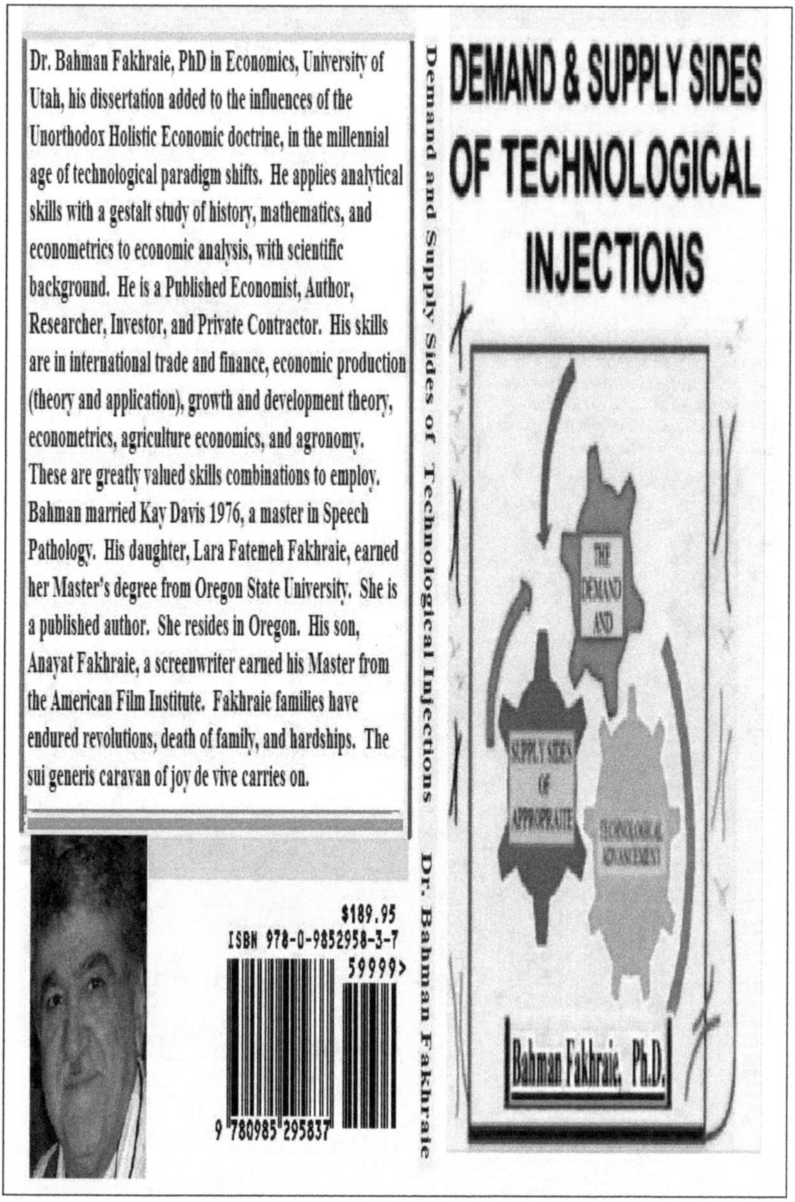
Dr. Bahman Fakhraie, PhD in Economics, University of Utah, his dissertation added to the influences of the Unorthodox Holistic Economic doctrine, in the millennial age of technological paradigm shifts. He applies analytical skills with a gestalt study of history, mathematics, and econometrics to economic analysis, with scientific background. He is a Published Economist, Author, Researcher, Investor, and Private Contractor. His skills are in international trade and finance, economic production (theory and application), growth and development theory, econometrics, agriculture economics, and agronomy. These are greatly valued skills combinations to employ. Bahman married Kay Davis 1976, a master in Speech Pathology. His daughter, Lara Fatemeh Fakhraie, earned her Master's degree from Oregon State University. She is a published author. She resides in Oregon. His son, Anayat Fakhraie, a screenwriter earned his Master from the American Film Institute. Fakhraie families have endured revolutions, death of family, and hardships. The sui generis caravan of joy de vive carries on.
$189.95
ISBN 978-0-9852958-3-7
59999>
9 780985 295837
Demand and Supply Sides of Technological Injections
Dr. Bahman Fakhraie
DEMAND & SUPPLY SIDES OF TECHNOLOGICAL INJECTIONS
THE DEMAND AND
SUPPLY SIDES OF APPROPRIATE
Bahman Fakhraie, Ph.D.

BOOK PROMO

Dr. Bahman Fakhraie, PhD in Economics, University of Utah, his dissertation added to the influences of the Unorthodox Holistic Economic doctrine, in the millennial age of technological paradigm shifts. He applies analytical skills with a gestalt study of history, mathematics, and econometrics to economic analysis, with scientific background. He is a Published Economist, Author, Researcher, Investor, and Private Contractor. His skills are in international trade and finance, economic production (theory and application), growth and development theory, econometrics, agriculture economics, and agronomy. These are greatly valued skills combinations to employ. Bahman married Kay Davis 1976, a master in Speech Pathology. His daughter, Lara Fatemeh Fakhraie, earned her Master's degree from Oregon State University. She is a published author. She resides in Oregon. His son, Anayat Fakhraie, a screenwriter earned his Master from the American Film Institute. Fakhraie families have endured revolutions, death of family, and hardships. The sui generis caravan of joy de vive carries on.
$349.99
ISBN 978-0-9852958-6-8
59999>
9 780985 295868
Dr. Bahman Fakhraie Teconomic Analysis of Cascading Millennial Economies
Teconomic Analysis of Cascading Millennial Economies
Technological Injections
TECONOMIC ANALYSIS
ANALYTICAL REMEDIES FOR
THE MILLENNIAL CASCADING ECONOMIES
Micro
Macro
Policy
Bahman Fakhraie, PhD

BOOK PROMO

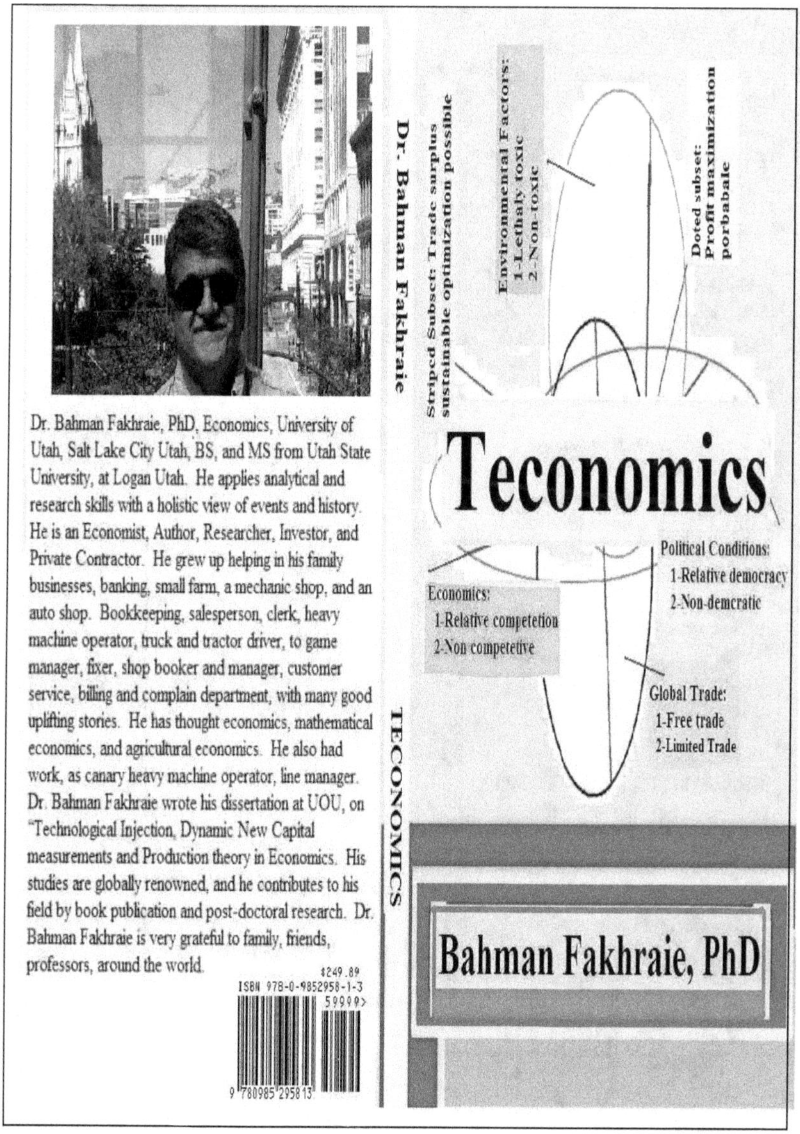
Dr. Bahman Fakhraie, PhD, Economics, University of Utah, Salt Lake City Utah, BS, and MS from Utah State University, at Logan Utah. He applies analytical and research skills with a holistic view of events and history. He is an Economist, Author, Researcher, Investor, and Private Contractor. He grew up helping in his family businesses, banking, small farm, a mechanic shop, and an auto shop. Bookkeeping, salesperson, clerk, heavy machine operator, truck and tractor driver, to game manager, fixer, shop booker and manager, customer service, billing and complain department, with many good uplifting stories. He has thought economics, mathematical economics, and agricultural economics. He also had work, as canary heavy machine operator, line manager. Dr. Bahman Fakhraie wrote his dissertation at UOU, on "Technological Injection, Dynamic New Capital measurements and Production theory in Economics. His studies are globally renowned, and he contributes to his field by book publication and post-doctoral research. Dr. Bahman Fakhraie is very grateful to family, friends, professors, around the world.
$249.89
ISBN 978-0-9852958-1-3
59999>
9 780985 295813
Dr. Bahman Fakhraie
TECONOMICS
Striped Subset: Trade surplus sustainable optimization possible
Environmental Factors:
1-Lethaly toxic
2-Non-toxic
Doted subset:
Profit maximization porbabale
Teconomics
Political Conditions:
1-Relative democracy
2-Non-demcratic
Economics:
1-Relative competetion
2-Non competetive
Global Trade:
1-Free trade
2-Limited Trade
Bahman Fakhraie, PhD

BOOK PROMO

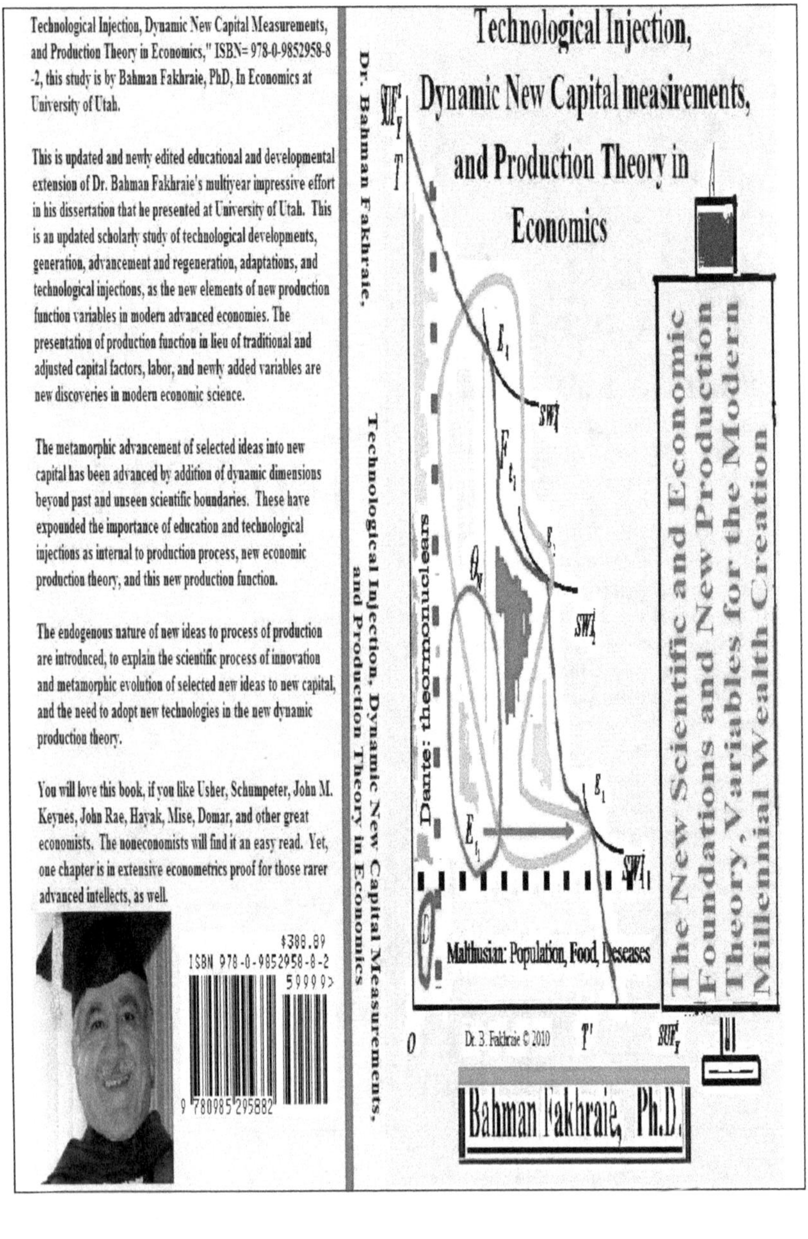
Technological Injection, Dynamic New Capital Measurements, and Production Theory in Economics," ISBN= 978-0-9852958-8 -2, this study is by Bahman Fakhraie, PhD, In Economics at University of Utah.
This is updated and newly edited educational and developmental extension of Dr. Bahman Fakhraie's multiyear impressive effort in his dissertation that he presented at University of Utah. This is an updated scholarly study of technological developments, generation, advancement and regeneration, adaptations, and technological injections, as the new elements of new production function variables in modern advanced economies. The presentation of production function in lieu of traditional and adjusted capital factors, labor, and newly added variables are new discoveries in modern economic science.
The metamorphic advancement of selected ideas into new capital has been advanced by addition of dynamic dimensions beyond past and unseen scientific boundaries. These have expounded the importance of education and technological injections as internal to production process, new economic production theory, and this new production function.
The endogenous nature of new ideas to process of production are introduced, to explain the scientific process of innovation and metamorphic evolution of selected new ideas to new capital, and the need to adopt new technologies in the new dynamic production theory.
You will love this book, if you like Usher, Schumpeter, John M. Keynes, John Rae, Hayak, Mise, Domar, and other great economists. The noneconomists will find it an easy read. Yet, one chapter is in extensive econometrics proof for those rarer advanced intellects, as well.
$388.89
ISBN 978-0-9852958-8-2
59999>
9 780985 295882
Dr. Bahman Fakhraie,
Technological Injection, Dynamic New Capital Measurements, and Production Theory in Economics
Technological Injection,
Dynamic New Capital measirements,
and Production Theory in
Economics
Dante: theomonuclears
Malthusian: Population, Food, Deseases
Dr. B. Fakhraie © 2010
The New Scientific and Economic Foundations and New Production Theory, Variables for the Modern Millennial Wealth Creation
Bahman Fakhraie, Ph.D.

Dr. Bahman Fakhraie, PhD in Economics, University of Utah, his dissertation added to the influences of the Unorthodox Holistic Economic doctrine, in the millennial age of technological paradigm shifts. He applies analytical skills with a gestalt study of history, mathematics, and econometrics to economic analysis, with scientific background. He is a Published Economist, Author, Researcher, Investor, and Private Contractor. His skills are in international trade and finance, economic production (theory and application), growth and development theory, econometrics, agriculture economics, and agronomy. These are greatly valued skills combinations to employ. Bahman married Kay Davis 1976, a master in Speech Pathology. His daughter, Lara Fatemeh Fakhraie, earned her Master's degree from Oregon State University. She is a published author. She resides in Oregon. His son, Anayat Fakhraie, a screenwriter earned his Master from the American Film Institute. Fakhraie families have endured revolutions, death of family, and hardships. The sui generis caravan of joy de vive carries on. Dr. Bahman Fakhraie was invited by Senator Frank M. Browning to attend Utah State University, when Senator visited his family. He has met most of modern day science and economic opinion leaders. Dr. Bahman Fakhraie's research yielded three books, (check the internet) , 1- THE DEMAND AND SUPPLY SIDES OF APPROPRIATE TECHNOLOGICAL INJECTIONS. 2- TECONOMIC ANALYSIS, ANALYTICAL REMEDIES FOR THE MILLENNIAL CASADING ECONOMIES. 3-TECONOMICS, Scientific Synthesis of Microeconomics and Technological injections in economics.

$80.00
ISBN 978-0-9966334-6-8
58000>
9 780996 633468

www.ingramcontent.com/pod-product-compliance
Lightning Source LLC
LaVergne TN
LVHW052224200926
848481LV00001B/210